Treasure for the Taking

Also by Anne Thaxter Eaton

READING WITH CHILDREN

THE ANIMALS' CHRISTMAS

TREASURE

FOR THE TAKING

A Book List
for Boys and Girls

BY

ANNE THAXTER EATON

———————————

THE VIKING PRESS

NEW YORK

1946

Foreword

Signposts on the highway are no substitute for a journey, and by the same token a list of books suggested for children's reading can be no substitute for a firsthand acquaintance with the books themselves. For children, the journey—that is, the book—is the chief consideration; and if the child who loves to read is surrounded by well-selected books within the range of his reading ability, he will soon find what he wants, whether it be a tale of magic and enchantment or an account of the latest rocket-ship. Children's books, however, are bought for children by adults; and with the multitude of books for boys and girls that are published every year, parents and others who are selecting books for children need some thread to guide them through the maze.

Then, too, a comprehensive book list reminds us who are older of books that delighted our own childhood, for the great children's books of the past, *Alice in Wonderland, The Wind in the Willows,* the *Just So Stories* and *The Jungle Book, Little Women* and *The Peterkin Papers,* Howard Pyle's *Robin Hood* and *The Wonder Clock,* are a priceless heritage which we pass on to children.

Book lists, to be of value, must be used intelligently. Even when age levels for the books are indicated, it must always be remembered that children of the same age differ materially in tastes, interests, and reading ability; and any grading of books according to age can only be tentative. A child's range is more often than not exceedingly wide, and every child and his reading must be considered as an individual case. There is, for instance, the eagerly reading little girl who essays serious adult fiction during the summer holidays and enjoys the experience, but who returns in September with content and pleasure to Mrs. Burnett's *The Secret Garden*. There are the high-school boys who relax with delighted chuckles over *The 500 Hats of Bartholomew Cubbins,* or sandwich Eleanor Hoffman's *Mischief in Fez* between a play by Maxwell Anderson and *They Were Expendable.*

A children's reading list, then, will suggest possible titles for books to be purchased to build up the personal library which is one of the most precious possessions of the growing boy or girl, or titles of books to be sought for in public or school library. It may be used to find books which will help boys and girls to pursue their hobbies and special interests; and, when a certain book has proved particularly appealing, to indicate more books of the same kind—richly imaginative tales, like Julia Sauer's *Fog Magic,* J. R. R. Tolkien's *The Hobbit,* Anne Parrish's *Floating Island,* or Christine Weston's *Bhimsa the Dancing Bear;* tales of lifelike children, such as Arthur Ransome's *Swallows and Amazons;* tales of present-day adventure, like Stephen Meader's *The Long Trains Roll;* stories of children of other lands, like Kate Seredy's *The Good Master;* and those that, like Elizabeth Janet Gray's *Adam of the Road,* illuminate the past.

Child and adult working together and in sympathy can choose a better book for the child's reading than either one can choose alone. Some adults have the gift of enjoying the imaginative story, the high-hearted legend, the tale of stirring adventure, with a child's whole-souled delight. If these fortunate adults take the opportunity to share books with boys and girls by reading aloud or by talking the books over, comparing and exchanging impressions, they will not only help these boys and girls to become real readers and true lovers of books, but they will secure for themselves an enriching experience.

Contents

CHAPTER I

Picture Books and Easy Reading

LONG before school days begin, boys and girls are ready for their first adventures in the world of books. Mother Goose, with her rhymes and jingles, will show them the way; verse by poets who understand childhood, Robert Louis Stevenson, A. A. Milne, Walter de la Mare, and others, furnishes enchanting music along the road. A host of delightful picture books awaits the young traveler, made by such contemporary artists as Leslie Brooke, Wanda Gág, Elsa Beskov, Kurt Wiese, and those first three famous makers of picture books, Randolph Caldecott, Walter Crane, and Kate Greenaway, all of whom see the world of imagination and the world of reality as the child sees them, fresh and gay and full of wonder. Soon comes the time when a child able to follow a connected story enjoys the old folk tales, the story of the Three Bears and Little Black Sambo, Pinocchio and Winnie-the-Pooh.

Mother Goose rhymes are a little child's introduction to poetry.

Mother Goose. *Little Mother Goose;* with numerous il. in full color and black and white by Jessie Willcox Smith. Dodd, 1918. Very popular because of its size, selection of rhymes, and attractive pictures. Ages 2–7.

Mother Goose. *Mother Goose, or The Old Nursery Rhymes;* il. in color by Kate Greenaway. Warne. This contains only a limited number of the rhymes, but its charming illustrations and small size make it a very pleasing volume to little children. Ages 2–7.

Mother Goose. *Mother Goose; Seventy-seven Verses;* with pictures by Tasha Tudor. Oxford, 1944. Gay and charming pictures in lovely color that make the Mother Goose country and its inhabitants a very real delight. Ages 3–6.

Mother Goose. *Mother Goose's Melodies, or Songs for the Nursery;* music given for nine of the melodies; ed. by W. A. Wheeler. Houghton. First published in 1878. A good collection, illustrated with old-fashioned woodcuts. Ages 2–7.

Mother Goose. *Mother Goose's Nursery Rhymes;* ed. by L. Edna Walter; il. by Charles Folkard. Macmillan, 1922. Comprehensive edition. Ages 2–6.

Mother Goose. *Nursery Rhyme Book;* ed. by Andrew Lang. Warne, 1897. One of the most complete collections for children's use. Delightfully illustrated by L. Leslie Brooke. Ages 2–7.

Mother Goose. *Ring o' Roses; a Nursery Rhyme Picture Book;* numerous drawings in color and black and white by L. Leslie Brooke. Warne. Mr. Brooke's inimitable full-page drawings in color make this one of the most desirable collections of Mother Goose rhymes for little children. Ages 2–7.

Aesop. *The Fables of Aesop;* selected, told anew, and their history traced by Joseph Jacobs. Macmillan, 1934. (Children's Classics.) An excellent edition, with spirited drawings in black and white by Richard Heighway. These brief, pointed tales of talking birds and beasts have a directness very satisfying to children. Ages 6–10.

Aesop. *Fables;* ed. and il. with wood engravings by Boris Artzybasheff. Viking, 1933. A beautiful, distinguished volume. Mr. Artzybasheff has illustrated carefully-selected versions of the *Fables* with wit and distinction. Age 10 on.

Ardizzone, Edward. *Little Tim and the Brave Sea Captain;* il. Oxford, 1936. An adventure story which the five- and six-year-old enjoys. The author wrote it and made the pictures, which have real beauty and catch the quality of the sea, for his own little son. Ages 5–8.

Artzybasheff, Boris. *Seven Simeons; a Russian Tale;* retold and il. by Boris Artzybasheff. Viking, 1937. A jolly story of seven peasants who with their magic aided their king. Illustrated with humor and a gay and flowing line. Ages 9–11.

Austin, Margot. *Peter Churchmouse;* written and il. by Margot Austin. Dutton, 1941. Pictures and story have a droll humor that is irresistible. The author's *Gabriel Churchkitten* (Dutton, 1942) tells more about Peter and his friends. Ages 5–8.

Bannerman, Helen. *Story of Little Black Sambo.* Stokes, 1923. Humorous, simple, and dramatic, this is a classic of childhood no boy or girl should miss. Ages 4–7.

Belpré, Pura. *Perez and Martina; a Porto Rican Folk Tale;* il. by Carlos Sanchez. Warne, 1932. A sprightly retelling of a droll folk tale. The full-page pictures in color have a fine quality of movement, and the book is full of gaiety and humor. Ages 7–8.

Bemelmans, Ludwig. *Quito Express;* il. by the author. Viking, 1938. A lovable, humorous little book about Pedro, the Inca baby, who was carried away by the fast Quito express. The author's characteristic drawings, in brown chalk, are delightful. Ages up to 10.

Beskov, Elsa. *Pelle's New Suit;* picture book, il. by the author; trans. from the Swedish by M. L. Woodburn. Harper, 1929. This shows how Pelle's new suit was made, from the shearing of his lamb through all the processes of cloth making. The lovely pictures in color make this one of the most appealing of the realistic picture-story books. Ages 5–8.

Beskov, Elsa. *Tale of the Wee Little Old Woman;* trans. from the Swedish by M. L. Woodburn. Harper, 1930. The very brief text and the author's lively pictures tell dramatically a story which little children find extremely funny. Ages 3–6.

Bianco, Mrs. Margery W. *Velveteen Rabbit, or How Toys Become Real.* Doubleday, 1926. William Nicholson's beautiful pictures help to make this story of a much-loved toy animal, who changes into a real one, very convincing. Ages 6–10.

Bishop, Claire Huchet. *Five Chinese Brothers;* il. by Kurt Wiese. Coward-McCann, 1938. Story and pictures are full of a spontaneous fun and a humorous exaggeration that children and their elders enjoy. Ages 5–8.

Boutet de Monvel, M. *Susanna's Auction;* from the French; il. by the author. Macmillan, 1923. (Little Library.) In this quaint little tale of a very real little girl of long ago, we find the naughtiness children so enjoy hearing about presented with humor and a moral. Ages 5–8.

Bransom, Paul and Fish, Helen Dean. *Animals of American History; a Picture Book.* Lippincott, 1939. Fifty black and white drawings of American animal life and a descriptive text interpret the part these animals have played in the American scene from the beginning. Ages 6–12.

Brooke, L. Leslie. *Golden Goose Book;* contains "The Golden Goose," "The Three Bears," "The Three Little Pigs," "Tom Thumb." Warne, 1906. The stories are also published separately. Mr. Brooke's drawings, full of action and humor, give fresh life to these old favorites. Ages 3–7.

Brooke, L. Leslie. *Johnny Crow's Garden.* Warne, 1904. Little children should not miss the gaiety and humor of this and the companion volumes, *Johnny Crow's Party* (Warne, 1907) and *Johnny Crow's New Garden* (Warne, 1935). Leslie Brooke's fun delights without confusing. Ages 2–6.

Brown, Beatrice Curtis. *Jonathan Bing, and Other Verses;* il. by Pelagie Doane. Oxford, 1936. The rhymes about this amiable, absent-minded old gentleman, who has great difficulty in managing the everyday affairs of life, make a strong appeal to children. Ages 5–8.

Brown, Margaret Wise. *The Little Fisherman;* il. by Dahlov Ipcar. Scott, 1945. With a fine feeling for design and color and an understanding of children's tastes, this young artist has drawn sea creatures, fishing boats, and fishermen to accompany a simple story which has the repetition boys and girls enjoy. Ages 4–7.

Buff, Mary and Conrad. *Dash and Dart;* with four oil paintings reproduced in full color and many black and white drawings by Conrad Buff. Viking, 1942. The story of two baby deer in the Southwest, told with a beautiful simplicity and deep feeling for wild life and the out-of-doors. Ages 5–10.

Burton, Virginia Lee. *The Little House;* story and pictures by Virginia Lee Burton. Houghton, 1942. An original and charming picture book that tells what happens as cities grow larger and encroach more and more on the green of fields and orchards. Ages 5–10.

Burton, Virginia Lee. *Katy and the Big Snow;* il. by the author. Houghton, 1943. How Katy, the red crawler tractor, plowed out the city in a blizzard is presented in delightful pictures and a brief text, with complete accuracy and an endearing humor. Ages 4–7.

Caldecott, Randolph. *The Farmer's Boy.* Warne. First published 1878. An excellent first picture book for a two-year-old. Caldecott's drawings have the lively action which delights the youngest children. The four *Caldecott Picture Books,* which in addition to "The Farmer's Boy" contain "John Gilpin," "The Babes in the Wood," "Hey Diddle Diddle," "The Frog He Would A-Wooing Go," "The Great Panjandrum Himself," and many more tales in verse, are not only an inexhaustible source of pleasure to children but provide an early training in the appreciation of fine draftsmanship. Ages 2–8.

Carrick, Valéry. *Picture Tales from the Russian;* trans. by N. Forbes. Stokes, 1913. These folk tales are told with simplicity and the same vigorous humor that characterizes the pictures. *More Russian Picture Tales* by the same author (Stokes, 1914) is equally satisfactory. Ages 5–9.

Chalmers, Audrey. *Birthday of Obash;* told and il. by Audrey Chalmers. Oxford, 1937. There is a childlike humor and spontaneity in this story of a baby hippopotamus who went in search of a birthday celebration and found one. The drawings are delightful. Ages 5–8.

Chalmers, Audrey. *Hundreds and Hundreds of Pancakes;* story and pictures by Audrey Chalmers. Viking, 1942. How Mrs. Frizzlewit calmed the animals who had escaped from the zoo during a cyclone by feeding them pancakes is told with engaging unforced humor. Ages 5–8.

Chalmers, Audrey. *I Had a Penny;* il. by the author. Viking, 1944. The little story in verse and the childlike drawings reflect the joyous feeling of adventure which a young child finds in doing the simple things of every day. Ages 4–6.

Chalmers, Audrey. *Poppadilly;* il. by the author. Viking, 1945. About a mouse who wanted to be big, a vain and selfish elf, and some magic poppy seeds. Full of fun and make-believe. Ages 5–8.

Charushin, E. *Baby Bears, a True Story;* trans. from the Russian by Marguerita Rudolph; il. by George Korff. Macmillan, 1944. A picture-story book with humor, genuine feeling for animals, and an authentic flavor of the north Russian country from which it comes. Ages 6–8.

Clark, Ann Nolan. *In My Mother's House;* il. by Velino Herrera. Viking, 1941. This book about the Tewa Indian children of the Tesuque pueblo near Santa Fe tells of everyday things with the poetry, simplicity, and directness of childhood. The pictures are made by a painter thoroughly familiar with Indian art and life. Ages 5–8.

Clark, Margery. *Poppy Seed Cakes;* il. by Maud and Miska Petersham. Doubleday, 1929. These gay pictures have an Old World flavor, and children find the adventures of Erminka and Andrewshek dramatic and amusing. Ages 5–7.

Collodi, Carlo. *Adventures of Pinocchio;* trans. from the Italian by C. M. Della Chiesa; il. in colors by Attilio Mussino. Macmillan, 1927. (Children's Classics.) Perennially popular with children are the adventures of the wooden marionette who came to life. Ages 6–10.

Crane, Walter. *The Baby's Opera; a Book of Old Rhymes with New Dresses;* the music by the earliest masters. Warne. Walter Crane's drawings make this a picture book, as well as a unique and charming songbook. Ages 2–5.

Daugherty, James H. *Andy and the Lion.* Viking, 1938. A new telling of the story of Androcles and the lion who got a thorn in his foot. A picture book with genuine humor, originality, and vigor. Ages 5–10.

D'Aulaire, Ingri and Edgar Parin. *Animals Everywhere*. Double-day, 1940. A gay panorama picture book showing animal life from the tropics to the Far North. Crayon lithographs in four colors display the animals of the cold, hot, and temperate zones in their native surroundings. Ages 2–5.

De Angeli, Marguerite. *Ted and Nina Go to the Grocery Store*. Doubleday, 1935. A cheerful little picture book telling how two children find adventure in going to the grocery store. *Ted and Nina Have a Happy Rainy Day* (Doubleday, 1936) tells of an afternoon spent in the attic "dressing up." Ages 6–8.

Ets, Marie Hall. *In the Forest;* il. by the author. Viking, 1944. A picture-story book with so much gaiety, humor, and imaginative insight that child and adult can share it with delight. Ages 4–7.

Falls, Charles. *A B C Book*. Doubleday, 1923. A fine animal alphabet book. Ages 3–5.

Farjeon, Eleanor. *A Prayer for Little Things;* pictures by Elizabeth Orton Jones. Houghton, 1945. (Nursery Books.) Twelve lovely pictures in color accompany the ten stanzas of a sensitive, childlike poem-prayer. Both little children and their mothers will feel the beauty of the book and the sense of security it gives. Other titles in this excellent series are: *Everyday Birds,* by Gertrude E. Allen; *Five and Ten,* by Roberta Whitehead; *Michael the Colt,* by Katharine Garbutt; *Muggins,* by Bianca Bradbury. Ages 2–5.

Ferrer, Melchor G. *Tito's Hats;* il. by Jean Charlot. Garden City Pub. Co., 1940. Beautiful line drawings and an amusing child-like story of a little Mexican boy. Ages 7–10.

Field, Rachel. *Prayer for a Child;* pictures by Elizabeth Orton Jones. Macmillan, 1944. This prayer in verse, written by Rachel Field for her small daughter, expresses a child's affection for people and for the simple everyday things around her. Beautiful pictures in color. Age 7 on.

Flack, Marjorie and Wiese, Kurt. *The Story about Ping*. Viking, 1933. This story of a Chinese duck who lived in a houseboat is full of drama and action. The pictures by Kurt Wiese, with their charm and gentle humor, make a strong appeal and convey the atmosphere of the country they describe. Ages 3–7.

Gág, Wanda. *The A B C Bunny;* hand-lettered by Howard Gág. Coward-McCann, 1933. Every letter of the alphabet provides an adventure for Bunny, who scampers gaily from A to Z. Wanda Gág's drawings are full of beauty and motion. Ages 2–5.

Gág, Wanda. *Millions of Cats.* Coward-McCann, 1928. This original picture-story book with its delightfully humorous drawings has the rhythmic repetition and sturdy quality of the folk tale. Ages 4–8.

Gramatky, Hardie. *Little Toot;* pictures by the author. Putnam, 1939. A gay little tale with light-hearted drawings of a fun-loving tug who awakened to a sense of responsibility. Children respond to the imaginative enjoyment with which the author-artist has drawn his tugs, ocean liners, and other craft. Ages 4–7.

Greenaway, Kate. *Under the Window; Pictures and Rhymes.* Warne. First published in 1879. Also, *Marigold Garden; Rhymes and Pictures.* Warne, 1880. The quaintly clad little boys and girls which this famous illustrator draws on the daisy-sprinkled turf and among the clipped evergreens of a formal garden are real children and are recognized as such by boys and girls of today. The verses have a gentle conciseness restful and pleasing to little children. Ages 5–7.

Grimm, J. L. K. and Grimm, W. K. *Snow White and the Seven Dwarfs;* freely trans. and il. by Wanda Gág. Coward-McCann, 1938. The best version for reading aloud to little children. The drawings catch completely the folk-tale atmosphere. Ages 6–9.

Handforth, Thomas. *Mei Li.* Doubleday, 1938. In this distinguished picture book, the author's beautiful drawings together with the imaginative, sympathetic story show us how a little girl of North China went to the Peiping Fair. Ages 6–8.

Hoffmann, Heinrich. *Slovenly Peter (Struwwelpeter)* taken direct from the original, reproducing the original colored illustrations. Winston. A famous old picture book enjoyed by many generations of children. The rhymes tell of the dire disasters which befall naughty children. Mark Twain made a free translation for his own children which was published by Harper in 1935. Ages 6–9.

Ivimey, John William. *The Complete Version of Ye Three Blind Mice;* il. by Walter Corbould. Warne, 1909. The original rhyme amplified until it makes a jolly story in verse which little children enjoy for its humor and dramatic quality. The pictures in color are spirited and amusing. Ages 2–6.

Johnson, Margaret S. and Helen Lossing. *The Smallest Puppy;* written and il. by Margaret S. Johnson and Helen Lossing Johnson. Harcourt, 1940. Simple story of an Eskimo puppy who, though he was the smallest of the family, was also the most enterprising. The large type is inviting to beginners in reading. Ages 5–9.

Kingman, Lee. *Pierre Pigeon;* with pictures by Arnold Edwin Bare. Houghton, 1943. The story of a small boy who lived in the Gaspé Peninsula in Canada, his Newfoundland dog, and his ship models. Simple, pleasing illustrations. Ages 7–9. *Ilenka,* by the same author, with gay pictures by Arnold Edwin Bare (Houghton, 1945), shows a busy Soviet town where a lively family of four children and their parents work and study and enjoy many good times. Ages 5–7.

Lathrop, Dorothy P. *Bouncing Betsy;* il. by the author. Macmillan, 1936. A gay story of a lonely pet lamb who learns to butt rabbits and woodchucks. The author's pictures of Betsy and her wild playmates are beautiful and accurate. Ages 5–9.

Lathrop, Dorothy P. *Who Goes There?;* il. by the author. Macmillan, 1935. Beautiful pictures of the little wild creatures who come to the picnic that two little children provide for them in the woods. Ages 6–8.

LeFèvre, Félicité. *The Cock, the Mouse and the Little Red Hen; an Old Tale Retold;* il. by Tony Sarg. Macrae-Smith, 1917. One of the best-loved folk tales, well retold, with spirited drawings in color. Ages 5–8.

Lenski, Lois. *The Little Farm*. Oxford, 1942. In a very brief text and in pictures that have a gentle humor and a fine simplicity, Lois Lenski's books about little Mr. Small present factual material with imagination and charm. *The Little Train* (1940), *The Little Auto* (1934), and *The Little Airplane* (Oxford, 1938) are also much loved by little children. Ages 6–8.

McCloskey, Robert. *Make Way for Ducklings;* il. by the author. Viking, 1941. A gay story with delightful pictures about Mr. and Mrs. Mallard and their family of eight ducklings, who live on an island in the Charles River and think nothing of marching composedly in a line through the Boston streets to the Public Gardens. Ages 6–8.

MacDonald, Golden. *Red Light Green Light;* il. by Leonard Weisgard. Doubleday, 1944. Safety education—"With the green light you go, with the red light you stop"—taught with originality, charm, and beautiful pictures. Ages 5–7.

MacIntyre, Elisabeth. *Ambrose Kangaroo; a Story That Never Ends*. Scribner, 1942. A light-hearted tale of a venturesome baby kangaroo. The artist-author's drawings in color show many other fascinating Australian creatures. Ages 3–6.

MacIntyre, Elisabeth. *Susan Who Lives in Australia;* il. by the author. Scribner, 1944. Billabongs, wallabies, and jackaroos, along with "mustering," boundary riding, and other activities of Australian life are all here in a rhymed text and gay water colors, making the young reader feel that he has really seen a bit of Susan's country. Ages 5–7.

Milne, A. A. *Winnie-the-Pooh;* il. by E. H. Shepard. Dutton, 1926. No one should miss these never-to-be-forgotten animal characters, Mr. Edward Bear, known as Winnie-the-Pooh, Piglet, Eeyore the Donkey, Kanga, and Tigger, and their delightfully absurd adventures with Christopher Robin in the Forest. *The House at Pooh Corner* (Dutton, 1928) contains further adventures. Ages 5–9.

Newberry, Clare Turlay. *Herbert the Lion;* pictures by the author; new enl. ed. Harper, 1939. A picture-story book in the true nonsense vein, children delight in its fun and absurdity. Ages 4–7.

Newberry, Clare Turlay. *Marshmallow;* story and pictures. Harper, 1942. Marshmallow was a baby bunny, and the story of his friendship with Oliver, a cat of middle-age, as Mrs. Newberry tells it in text and pictures is a rare combination of beauty, humor, and understanding of children and animals. Ages 5–9.

Olds, Elizabeth. *The Big Fire;* il. by the author. Houghton, 1945. A history of the development of fire departments and fire equipment; a stirring account of a big city fire; splendid pictures in color of the engines and the men in action, and accurate drawings of the equipment. Ages 6–10.

Payne, Emily. *Katy No-Pocket;* pictures by H. A. Rey. Houghton, 1944. An hilarious tale of a kangaroo without a pocket in which to carry her baby, and her solution of the problem. Pictures in strong colors full of action and humor. Ages 6–8.

Payne, Josephine Balfour. *Once There Was Olga;* il. by Joan Balfour Payne. Putnam, 1944. Good-humored little story of a donkey, which has in text and pictures the homely, earthy quality of the folk tale. Ages 6–8.

Petersham, Maud and Miska. *The Rooster Crows; American Rhymes for America's Children.* Macmillan, 1945. Here are many jingles, nursery rhymes, counting-out games, skipping-rope songs, and others beloved by many generations of children, illustrated with gay and lively pictures. Ages 6–12.

Rey, H. A. *Cecily G. and the 9 Monkeys.* Houghton, 1942. A spirited picture-story book about an amiable giraffe and her monkey friends which delights children by its lively action and unforced humor. The author's *Curious George* (Houghton, 1941) who appears again as one of the nine monkeys is equally successful. Ages 3–6.

Rickert, Edith. *Bojabi Tree;* pictures by Gleb Botkin. Doubleday, 1923. Adapted from an African folk tale, this has the repetition, the humor, and the dramatic quality that little children enjoy. Ages 3–7.

Sayers, Frances Clarke. *Bluebonnets for Lucinda;* il. by Helen Sewell. Viking, 1934. A charming story of a real little girl, against an authentic background of Texas country. Ages 4–7.

Scudder, Horace E. *The Children's Book: A Collection of the Best and Most Famous Stories and Poems in the English Language;* new ed. Houghton, 1903. A book that should be in every household where there are children, for it will last through childhood and prove a treasure house into which the whole family may dip for years, finding it almost a complete library in itself. Ages 5–14.

Seuss, Dr. (T. S. Geisel). *And to Think That I Saw It on Mulberry Street;* il. by the author. Vanguard, 1937. This picture-story book in rhyme is true to the working of a child's imagination. Ages 4–8.

Sewell, Helen. *Blue Barns; the Story of Two Big Geese and Seven Little Ducks.* Macmillan, 1933. The tale is simple and direct, and the drawings have a quiet beauty. Ages 3–6.

Smith, E. Boyd. *The Chicken World;* drawn by E. Boyd Smith. Putnam, 1910. A fascinating picture book much loved by children, which describes the events in the lives of a busy hen and her growing children. In *The Farm Book* by this artist-author, the experiences of two city children on a farm are set forth in beautiful full-page pictures and a brief text. Houghton, 1910. Ages 4–8.

Smith, E. Boyd. *The Story of Noah's Ark;* told and pictured by E. B. Smith. Houghton, 1909. *After They Came Out of the Ark.* Putnam, 1930. Two delightful picture books. Mr. Smith has drawn the animals, in the ark and after they disembark in a visibly damp world, with humor and a touch of gentle satire that both children and adults enjoy. Ages 7–9.

Swift, Hildegarde H. and Ward, Lynd. *The Little Red Lighthouse and the Great Gray Bridge;* il. by Lynd Ward. Harcourt, 1942. A story that enters into a child's imaginative feeling about ferryboats, tugboats, and lighthouses. Lynd Ward's fine drawings have real power. Ages 4–6.

Townend, Jack. *Railroad A B C;* il. by Denison Budd. Watts, 1945. All the details of trains and signals and tracks are clearly shown in bright colors in this small, appealing book. Ages 4–6.

Wells, Rhea. *Peppi the Duck;* written and il. by Rhea Wells. Doubleday, 1927. This biography of a little duck born in a castle courtyard is treated with a gentle seriousness and illustrated with many engaging pictures in color and in black and white. Ages 6–9.

White, Eliza Orne. *Ann Frances;* il. by Helen Sewell. Houghton, 1935. This and *When Molly Was Six,* by the same author (Houghton, 1894), are excellent realistic stories with fine characterization. Ages 6–8.

Wiese, Kurt. *The Rabbit's Revenge;* written and il. by Kurt Wiese. Coward-McCann, 1940. Forty-eight genuinely funny pictures and a brief text show how a daring group of rabbits manage to circumvent Old Man Shivers's scheme to make himself a suit lined with rabbit's fur. *Karoo the Kangaroo,* by the same author-artist (Coward-McCann, 1929), tells of the life of a little kangaroo in his native forests. Ages 5–8.

Wiese, Kurt. *You Can Write Chinese;* il. by the author. Viking, 1945. Pictures of the Chinese characters and the forms from which they sprang make a beautiful and enlightening book. For all ages.

Williams, Gweneira. *Timid Timothy;* il. by Leonard Weisgard. W. R. Scott, 1944. Simple story and amusing pictures of a timid kitten who learns to be brave. Ages 3–5.

Zolotow, Charlotte. *The Park Book;* pictures by H. A. Rey. Harper, 1944. In a simple, friendly text and lively pictures in color, the passing scene of life in the park is made very real from early morning till the lights are lit at night. A picture book that will please both the children who are familiar with parks and those who are not. Ages 6–8.

CHAPTER II

Bible and Bible Stories

A CHILD who does not hear the Bible read aloud suffers an irreparable loss. Even though he may not understand the meaning completely, the Bible language, with its majesty and music, rings in his mind long afterward, building a foundation for the appreciation of beauty and rhythm in word and phrase.

For this reason books of Bible stories designed for children are more satisfactory when the editing consists of selection and omission rather than retelling. The following keep the language of the King James version.

Bible. *First Bible;* il. by Helen Sewell; sel. and arr. by J. W. Maury. Oxford, 1934. Here are the stories from the Old and the New Testament which time has proved to be the most interesting and inspiring to boys and girls. Helen Sewell's thirteen full-page drawings, in their reverent simplicity, rise to a high level of strength and beauty. Ages 7–12.

Bible. *Bible Stories to Read and Tell, One Hundred and Fifty Stories from the Old Testament;* sel. and arr. by F. J. Olcott; il. by Willy Pogány. Houghton, 1916. Edited by omitting a few words and an occasional passage. Ages 9–13.

Bible. *The Book of Books; the King James Version of the English Bible,* abridged and arranged with editorial comments for younger readers by W. O. Sypherd. Knopf, 1944. "A substantial part of the writings of the Old Testament and the New Testament which every educated boy and girl should know." Beautiful in design and typography. Ages 12–15.

Bible. *Small Rain;* selections from the Bible chosen by Jessie Orton Jones; il. by Elizabeth Orton Jones. Viking, 1943. Verses from the Bible, illustrated for children in childlike, appealing drawings of everyday American boys and girls. Ages 5–10.

CHAPTER III

Books About Religion

Fitch, Florence Mary. *One God; the Ways We Worship Him;* photographs selected by Beatrice Creighton. Lothrop, 1944. In explaining the three great religions of America and the way we worship God in this country, the author emphasizes not their differences but their common belief in one God. Ages 10–14.

Hogarth, Grace Allen. *A Bible A B C.* Stokes, 1941. A very simple religious book for the youngest children. The pictures have exactly the right amount of detail to arouse a child's interest, never enough to confuse him. The mood varies, as does a child's mood; "A for Ark" and "W for Whale" sparkle with gaiety and humor; "Xmas," showing the Child and the animals, has gravity and tenderness. Ages 2–7.

Lathrop, Dorothy P. *Animals of the Bible;* a picture book by D. P. Lathrop, with text selected by Helen Dean Fish from the King James Bible. Stokes, 1937. This is more than a beautiful picture book, for Dorothy Lathrop has studied the fauna and flora of Bible lands until each animal and bird, each flower and tree, is true to natural history. Ages 5–9.

Petersham, Maud and Miska. *The Christ Child; As Told by Matthew and Luke;* il. by Maud and Miska Petersham. Doubleday, 1931. This is the Christmas story as told in the Gospels. The pictures, in lovely colors, have a childlike and beautiful simplicity. Ages 5–10.

Smith, Ruth. *The Tree of Life; Selections from the Literature of the World's Religions;* with an introduction by R. O. Ballou; il. by Boris Artzybasheff. Viking, 1942. Selected writings from the following religious faiths: American Indian, Norse, Hindu, Buddhist, Confucianist, Taoist, Egyptian, Babylonian, Greek, Zoroastrian, Hebrew and Christian, Mohammedan. There are introductory notes on background material. Ages 12–15.

CHAPTER IV

Talking Beasts and Other Fanciful Creatures

The fanciful animal story is akin to the fairy tale; often, however, it makes an earlier appeal. Some of the most delightful imaginative writing for children is to be found among these tales of talking beasts and other creatures who carry on their lives and conduct their affairs in a world which is neither the real world nor fairyland, but a world in which children feel themselves at home.

Baker, Margaret. *The Black Cats and the Tinker's Wife;* il. by Mary Baker. Dodd, 1923. A charming story with a folklore flavor, delightfully illustrated with silhouettes. *Tomson's Hallowe'en* (Dodd, 1929), by the same author and illustrator, is a gay and sprightly tale about a kindly witch who stays at home while Tomson, the cat, and the broom join the revelers. *Three for an Acorn* (Dodd, 1935) is a humorous account of how Mr. and Mrs. Squirrel tried to get their winter nuts without gathering them. Ages 7–9.

Bianco, Mrs. Margery W. *The Good Friends;* with lithographs by Grace Paull. Viking, 1934. A group of animals, Rhoda the Jersey Cow, Fanny and Billy the horses, Mrs. Happy and her kittens, Rufus the hound, and Rosie the irrepressible little goat, keep house by themselves while their owner is in the hospital. The author has characterized them skillfully and described their doings in a fine spirit of light-hearted make-believe. Ages 8–11.

Casserley, Anne. *Barney the Donkey;* pictures by the author. Harper, 1932. This mischievous but lovable animal hero is very appealing, and the stories are concerned with simple everyday matters of immediate interest to children. Ages 7–9.

Coatsworth, Elizabeth. *The Cat Who Went to Heaven;* il. by Lynd Ward. Macmillan, 1930. In this lovely, imaginative story there is something of the serenity of the East and the gentleness of a religion in which there is a place for the humblest of living creatures. Ages 9–12.

Ets, Marie Hall. *Mr. Penny;* il. by the author. Viking, 1935. A delightful bit of nonsense about the farm animals who were so grateful for Mr. Penny's good care that when he needed their help they took care of him. Ages 7–9.

Grahame, Kenneth. *The Wind in the Willows;* il. by E. H. Shepard. Scribner, 1933. The humor, intelligent absurdity, the kindly wisdom, and the poetry of this incomparable tale of Water Rat, Mole, Toad, Badger, and other animals who lived along the river bank or in the forest, give it an ageless and universal appeal. A book for the child and adult to enjoy together. Ages 9–15 and on.

Harris, Joel Chandler. *Uncle Remus, His Songs and Sayings;* new and rev. ed. with 112 il. by A. B. Frost, Appleton-Century, 1935. First published 1880. These stories told by an old negro, Uncle Remus, to a little boy on a southern plantation have a humor that is deep and genuine, and a spontaneity and joy in storytelling that belongs to the American Negro. No child should miss the pranks and carryings-on of Brer Rabbit, Brer Fox, Brer Wolf, Sis Cow, and the rest of the characters in this great piece of American literature. A good book for family reading aloud. Ages 8–15 and on.

Hatch, Richard W. *The Curious Lobster;* il. by Marion Freeman Wakeman. Harcourt, 1937. A fine, spontaneous tale full of the delightfully absurd logic which is the charm of the fanciful animal story. Followed by *The Curious Lobster's Island.* Dodd, Mead, 1939. Ages 8–10.

Kipling, Rudyard. *The Jungle Book;* il. by Kurt Wiese. Doubleday, 1932. Stories of Mowgli, the boy whom the wolves adopted, of Bagheera, the black panther, and Baloo, the bear; of Shere Khan, the tiger who sought Mowgli's life and lost his own, of Toomai of the Elephants, of Rikki Tikki, the Mongoose, and Kotick, the white seal. Kipling pictures animal life with truth and with the magic of imagination. Ages 8–15.

Kipling, Rudyard. *Just So Stories;* il. by J. M. Gleeson. Double-day, 1912. No child should miss these stories with their captivating and preposterous natural history explaining how the elephant got his trunk, the camel his hump, the leopard his spots, and why the cat walks by himself. The author's amazing and magnificent use of words is fascinating to boys and girls. A book to be read aloud. Ages 6–10.

Lagerlöf, Selma. *Wonderful Adventures of Nils;* trans. from the Swedish by V. S. Howard. Doubleday, 1907. This story of a human boy changed to an elf who journeys over Sweden with the wild geese and the tame white gander, the latter becoming the boy's special friend and companion, is full of charm and outdoor atmosphere. Ages 9–12.

Lawson, Robert. *Rabbit Hill;* il. by the author. Viking, 1944. This story of the small animals of the Connecticut fields and woods who shared the author's garden is compact of beauty and fun, kindliness, imaginative understanding, and love for the American countryside. All ages.

Lofting, Hugh. *Story of Doctor Dolittle; Being the Story of His Peculiar Life at Home and Astonishing Adventures in Foreign Parts. Never Before Printed.* Il. by the author. Stokes, 1920. The author of this story of a kind-hearted doctor who loves animals and understands their language enjoys make-believe in the same way that children do. There are other Dr. Dolittle books equally popular with boys and girls. The pictures are as full of humor as the text. Ages 8–11.

Peck, Leigh. *Don Coyote;* il. by Virginia Lee Burton. Houghton, 1942. Gathered from the Indians and Mexicans in the Southwest, these tales of Don Coyote, wisest of all the animals, are retold with spirit and humor, and Virginia Lee Burton has supplied notable illustrations. Ages 8–10.

Potter, Beatrix. *Fairy Caravan.* McKay, 1929. Fairies play a part in this story, but for the most part it concerns itself with guinea pigs, ferrets, ponies, Highland terriers, and a dormouse named Xarifa, against a delightful outdoor background. Ages 9–10.

Potter, Beatrix. *Tale of Peter Rabbit.* Warne, 1903. Peter Rabbit series (Warne, 1903–14, 18 vol.) includes also "Benjamin

Bunny," "Mrs. Tiggy Winkle," "Jemima Puddleduck," "Jeremy Fisher," and others. Beatrix Potter's beautifully written little stories and inimitable drawings have brought to life a whole exquisite society of small creatures. Ages 3–8.

Sayers, Frances Clarke. *Mr. Tidy Paws;* il. by Zhenya Gay. Viking, 1935. This fresh, original story of a strange little cat, of a village that moved and changed its name, of a little boy and his grandmother who stayed behind in the deserted town of Bean Blossom, is a mixture of the real and unreal which children find delightful. Ages 8–10.

CHAPTER V

Dogs and Cats

CHILDREN feel happily at home with these friendly, everyday creatures whose doings provide a never failing source of interest.

Bacon, Frances Atchinson. *Kitty Come Down;* pictures by Eloise Wilkin. Oxford, 1944. A friendly, amusing little story of a kitten who was frightened into running up a tree and how the distracted Morrow family spent three days trying to get their pet down again. Ages 6–9.

Chalmers, Audrey. *Fancy Be Good;* written and il. by Audrey Chalmers. Viking, 1941. A tale about twin kittens, one of whom was good and one bad, with irresistible drawings full of kitten-mischief and charm. Ages 6–9.

Cook, Gladys Emerson. *American Champions;* il. by the author. Macmillan, 1945. A picture book of famous dogs, each one a champion of his breed; a brief text notes important characteristics. Ages 8–15.

Davis, Mary Gould. *Sandy's Kingdom;* drawings by E. L. Brock. Harcourt, 1935. A real farm in Maine serves as background for this tale of a wise shepherd dog who was the guardian of the silver foxes. Ages 8–10.

Dennis, Morgan. *Burlap;* il. by the author. Viking, 1945. Many lively drawings and an amusing tale setting forth the adventures and misadventures of this lovably absurd Basset hound. Ages 6–10.

Goodman, Jack, ed. *The Fireside Book of Dog Stories;* with an introduction by James Thurber. Simon, 1943. Thirty-nine dog stories. A book the whole family will enjoy. Age 9 on.

Hoffmann, Eleanor. *A Cat of Paris;* il. by Zhenya Gay. Stokes, 1940. People and events seen through the eyes of an absurd, lovable Siamese kitten against an authentic background of prewar Paris. Zhenya Gay's drawings have the same humor and liveliness as the story. Ages 8–12.

Johnson, Margaret S. and Helen Lossing. *Barney of the North;* written and il. by Margaret S. Johnson and Helen Lossing Johnson. Harcourt, 1939. The story of a Newfoundland puppy who twice proves himself a hero. The author-artists have written many other dog stories all admirably illustrated. Ages 7–9.

Kjelgaard, Jim. *Big Red;* il. by Bob Kuhn. Holiday House, 1945. The story of a champion Irish setter and a boy who knew how to handle him. Ages 12–15.

Knight, Eric. *Lassie Come-Home;* il. by Marguerite Kirmse. Winston, 1940. A thrilling story of a collie's four-hundred-mile journey back to the family she loved, after they had been forced to sell her. Ages 9–14.

Knight, Ruth Adams, *Valiant Comrades; a Story of Our Dogs of War.* Doubleday, 1943. The testing and training of dogs for war service is described in this interesting story. Ages 10–14.

L'Hommedieu, Dorothy K. *Tinker, the Little Fox Terrier;* il. by Marguerite Kirmse. Lippincott, 1942. The fine pictures make the dog hero of this pleasant, simple little story very real. Also, *Nipper, the Little Bull Pup;* il. by Marguerite Kirmse. Lippincott, 1943. Ages 6–8.

Lathrop, Dorothy P. *Puppies for Keeps;* il. by the author. Macmillan, 1943. Beautiful pictures, by a master in the art of drawing animals, that show the development of a family of four Pekingese puppies from their very first day till they could play with a ball and roll one another over. The text tells a satisfying little story of how the family, unable to agree on which puppy they could bear to give up, decided to keep them all. Age 7 on.

Lathrop, West. *Juneau, the Sleigh Dog;* il. by Kurt Wiese. Random House, 1942. A stirring adventure story and the portrait of a great dog. Ages 9–14.

Lippincott, Joseph Wharton. *Wilderness Champion;* il. by Paul Bransom. Lippincott, 1944. Stirring story of a red hound-pup lost in the Alberta mountains, a wolf of great valor, and a ranger who knew dogs as well as he knew his mountains. Ages 9–15.

London, Jack. *The Call of the Wild;* il. by Paul Bransom. Macmillan, 1929. Also, *White Fang,* Macmillan. These two stories portray splendid dogs and the wild country which was their background with reality and truth. Ages 9–15.

Machetanz, Frederick. *Panuck, Eskimo Sled Dog;* il. by the author in color and in black and white. Scribner, 1939. The story of the training of an Eskimo sled dog and how he rescued his master in a blizzard. The author knows the North. Fine illustrations. Ages 8–10.

Mason, Miriam E. *Matilda and Her Family;* il. by Meg Wohlberg. Macmillan, 1942. A story full of humor; for the author, who understands cats, tells her tale consistently from the cat's point of view. Pleasing illustrations. Ages 5–8. *Timothy Has Ideas,* il. by Berta and Elmer Hader (Macmillan, 1943), is the story of a cocker puppy written with a gentle humor and an understanding of all that a pet means in a child's life. Ages 7–9.

Meader, Stephen. *Bat, the Story of a Bull Terrier;* il. by Edward Shenton. Harcourt, 1939. Dramatic tale of a fine dog who was stolen but whose courage and instincts brought him safely home. Ages 9–13. *Skippy's Family,* il. by Elizabeth P. Korn (Harcourt, 1945), is Mr. Meader's sympathetic and humorous account of "a small, brown mongrel dog who for seventeen years was a full-fledged member of the family to whom he belonged." Ages 8–12.

Newberry, Clare Turlay. *Mittens;* il. by the author. Harper, 1936. Captivating pictures which have caught the very essence of kitten charm. Ages 5–8.

Ollivant, Alfred. *Bob, Son of Battle*. Doubleday, 1898. In this fine story of a champion sheep dog of the Dale, both dogs and human beings are drawn with skill and understanding. Ages 10–15.

Robinson, Tom. *Buttons;* drawings by Peggy Bacon. Viking, 1938. Peggy Bacon has made inimitable drawings for this entirely delightful and convincing tale about an alley cat who became a gentleman. Ages 5–8.

Robinson, Tom. *Pete;* il. by Morgan Dennis. Viking, 1941. Informal, humorous, and genuine, this story shows us dog nature and human nature at their best. Admirable illustrations. Ages 9–13.

Rubicam, Harry C. *Two-Spot, Wolf Dog of the Circle Y;* il. by Frederick T. Chapman. Knopf, 1941. Humorous tale of ranch life, in which both the dog and the men he lived with ring true. Ages 10–15.

Shepard, Birsa. *The Cat Next Door;* pictures by Pelagie Doane. Oxford, 1943. All little girls who love cats will be delighted with this tale of how Mollie found homes for five kittens so that not a single one had to be drowned. Ages 7–10.

Terhune, Albert Payson. *Lad, a Dog;* il. by R. L. Dickey. Dutton, 1926. The tale of a real dog who was the author's companion for years. Ages 10–14.

CHAPTER VI

Horses

ROMANCE still lives, for boys and girls, in horses and their stories.

Anderson, C. W. *Black, Bay and Chestnut: Profiles of Twenty Favorite Horses.* Macmillan, 1939. Twenty-two full-page pictures of famous or well-loved horses with a short description of the life and character of each one. Other popular books by this author are *Thoroughbreds, Deep Through the Heart,* and *A Touch of Greatness;* while his stories of a little boy and his pony, *Billy and Blaze,* and others (Macmillan) are favorites with younger children. *Big Red,* il. with lithographs by the author (Macmillan, 1943), gives the history and describes the personality of a great horse, "Man o' War." Ages 9–14.

Anderson, C. W. *Heads Up—Heels Down: A Handbook of Horsemanship and Riding;* il. by the author. Macmillan, 1944. Fundamental instruction on the riding and handling of horses, with many pictures. Ages 11–15.

Barrett, Lawrence. *Twinkle, the Baby Colt;* il. by the author. Knopf, 1945. Delightful pictures and a brief text catch the gay liveliness and endearing awkwardness of a colt. Ages 4–8.

Dennis, Wesley. *Flip;* story and pictures by Wesley Dennis. Viking, 1941. Thoroughly delightful pictures and an engaging story make this little colt very real. Followed by *Flip and the Cows.* Viking, 1942. Ages 5–8.

Garrard, Phyllis. *Running Away with Nebby;* il. by Willy Pogány. McKay, 1944. When Noel and Marigold decide to keep their beloved dapple-gray horse from being sold, they embark on a series of adventures which, if slightly improbable, are described with an engaging zest. Ages 8–12.

Golden Gorse, pseud. *Moorland Mousie;* il. by Lionel Edwards. Scribner, 1930. Well-written story of an Exmoor pony, with sixteen plates by an artist whose pictures of horses are deservedly famous. A sequel, *Older Mousie,* is also illustrated by Mr. Edwards. Ages 9–12.

Hader, Berta and Elmer. *Spunky, the Story of a Shetland Pony.* Macmillan, 1933. The life of a wild pony who went first to the mines, then across the Atlantic, and finally joined a circus. Fine pictures. Ages 9–11.

Henry, Marguerite. *Justin Morgan Had a Horse;* il. by Wesley Dennis. Wilcox and Follett, 1945. Justin Morgan was the schoolteacher who took the little colt nobody wanted, a colt that grew up to be the first in a long line of American horses, the famous Morgan breed. Ages 9–12.

Hinkle, Thomas C. *Black Storm, a Horse of the Kansas Hills.* Morrow, 1929. A story based on fact, of a high-hearted horse and a high-hearted man and the friendship between them. Ages 9–15.

James, Will. *Smoky the Cowhorse.* Scribner, 1926. In his drawings and stories Will James has preserved for all time the horses of the cattle country. Ages 9–15.

Johnson, Margaret S. and Helen Lossing. *Stablemates, the Story of Dick and Daisy;* written and il. by Margaret S. Johnson and Helen Lossing Johnson. Harcourt, 1942. The story of two colts born on a Virginia plantation and their devotion to one another, illustrated with charm and sympathy. Ages 6–9.

O'Hara, Mary. *My Friend Flicka.* Lippincott, 1941. (Story Press Book.) A stirring story of the friendship between a boy and a horse. Ages 12–15.

Rounds, Glen. *The Blind Colt;* written and il. by Glen Rounds. Holiday House, 1941. Sympathetic story of how Whitey trained an intelligent colt, born blind, to be his "Sunday horse." Good picture of the West. Ages 9–12.

Sewell, Anna. *Black Beauty;* with il. of the late nineteenth century by John Beer, together with an introductory biographical sketch of the author. Dodd, 1941. (Great Illustrated Classics.) First published in 1877, this still retains its hold on children's affections. Ages 9–11.

Watson, Helen Orr. *Shavetail Sam, U.S. Army Mule;* il. by Bernard Garbutt. Houghton, 1944. The story of an army mule who is not only intelligent but has a sense of humor. Authentic background of army life in wartime. Ages 9–14.

Watson, Helen Orr. *Top Kick, U.S. Army Horse;* il. by Bernard Garbutt. Houghton, 1942. A good story of the training and service of an army horse, by an author who knows army life and military posts. The illustrator knows and loves horses and draws them well. Ages 9–14.

CHAPTER VII

Pets

Bianco, Mrs. Margery W. *All about Pets;* decorations by Grace Gilkinson. Macmillan, 1929. Children who love animals will find this book not only useful but fun to read. Ages 9–12.

Comstock, Anna B. *The Pet Book.* Comstock Pub. Co., 1914. Useful information on the care of many kinds of pets. Ages 10–14.

CHAPTER VIII

Wild Animals Everywhere

Boys and girls following the lives and experiences of wild animals in books find themselves adventuring all over the world, from Arctic seas to tropical jungles.

Atkinson, Agnes Akin. *Perkey, a Biography of a Skunk;* with twenty-three photographs by S. R. Atkinson. Viking, 1937. Mr. and Mrs. Atkinson live near the foot of Mt. Wilson on the edge of the National Forest, and this and several other animal biographies have been written from their observation of the wild creatures who find their way to the feeding table in the Atkinsons' back yard. Ages 9–11.

Baynes, Ernest H. *The Sprite, the Story of a Red Fox;* many photographs by Louise Birt Baynes and the author; introd. by Dallas Lore Sharp. Macmillan, 1924. This and *Jimmie, the Story of a Black Bear Cub* (Macmillan, 1923) are delightful stories, by a true animal lover, of animals kept as pets. Ages 10–13.

Bronson, Wilfrid S. *Horns and Antlers;* il. by the author. Harcourt, 1942. Habits and life histories are given for deer, moose, reindeer, caribou, antelope, and mountain "goat." Clever and scientifically accurate drawings. Ages 9–12.

Ditmars, Raymond L. *Strange Animals I Have Known.* Harcourt, 1931. Fascinating stories of a naturalist's experiences. Ages 12–15.

Ditmars, Raymond L. *Twenty Little Pets from Everywhere;* il. by Helène Carter. Messner, 1943. Distinctive pictures and readable, informal text describe unusual pets of many different lands, including the panda, dormouse, lemming, cacomistle, jaguarundi, coati-mundi and others. Ages 8–10.

Drummond, Henry. *The Monkey Who Would Not Kill;* il. by Lois Lenski. Dodd, 1925. First published in 1897, this story of the antics of a mischievous monkey who "won't hang, won't drown, won't shoot," has been loved by children ever since. Ages 7–10.

Eberle, Irmengarde. *A Family to Raise;* pictures by Else Bostelmann. Holiday House, 1939. The home lives of the opossum, screech owl, snapping turtle, and others, described with dignity and understanding of the young child's interests. Ages 8–10.

Gall, Mrs. Alice C. and Crew, Fleming H. *All the Year Round;* pictures by Else Bostelmann. Oxford, 1944. These eight stories of small creatures, raccoon, ground hog, woodpecker, and others, two for each season, are written with sound knowledge and imaginative understanding of how a child feels toward animals and the outdoor world. Ages 5–8.

Gall, Mrs. Alice C. and Crew, Fleming H. *Flat Tail;* il. by W. Langdon Kihn. Oxford, 1935. This describes the second and most interesting year in a beaver family's life when, driven from their home by a forest fire, they build a dam and start a new colony. Beautiful pictures. The same authors have written a pleasing story of a tadpole in *Wagtail* (Oxford, 1932), and of a raccoon in *Ringtail* (Oxford, 1933). Ages 8–10.

Hegner, Robert W. and Mrs. Jane Z. *Parade of the Animal Kingdom.* Macmillan, 1935. In lively, readable style the authors describe the appearance and habits of a great number of animals, from the protozoon to the monkey, using 700 photographs as illustrations. Ages 12–15.

Hogner, Dorothy Childs and Nils. *The Animal Book; American Mammals North of Mexico;* text by Dorothy Childs Hogner and il. by Nils Hogner. Oxford, 1942. The characteristics, habits, and habitats of 170 American mammals north of Mexico are described in a style that is direct and vivid. The many illustrations add interest to the book. Ages 9–12.

Huey, Edward Greene. *Child's Story of the Animal World;* il. by H. R. Daugherty and Olive Earle. Reynal, 1935. Much information is given in easy readable chapters, with many pictures. Ages 9–12.

Johnson, Osa. *Tarnish, the True Story of a Lion Cub;* il. by Arthur August Jansson. Wilson and Follett, 1945. Outstanding among animal stories for the younger children because the author knows lions at first hand and has evoked from her own past experience something of the beauty and grandeur of the jungle, as a background for her tale of a blind, furry yellow kitten who learned to hunt and defend himself until he was ready to join the "pride of lions" to which his parents belonged. The illustrations are stirring and beautiful. Ages 7–9.

McCracken, Harold. *The Biggest Bear on Earth;* il. by Paul Bransom. Stokes, 1943. A dignified, interesting account of the Alaskan brown bears, based on a naturalist's firsthand observation. The author's *The Son of the Walrus King,* il. by Lynn Bogue Hunt (Lippincott, 1944), draws a vivid picture of Arctic animals. Ages 9–12.

McCracken, Harold. *The Last of the Sea Otters;* with drawings by Paul Bransom. Stokes, 1942. The life cycle of the sea otter, beautifully told. Based on the author's personal observation and experience in the Aleutian islands. Ages 10–13.

Mason, George F. *Animal Tracks;* il. by the author. Morrow, 1943. The pictures of forty-four North American mammals, with their tracks and footprints, and a brief text. Prepared by a staff artist of the American Museum of Natural History as an aid in the identification of animal tracks. Age 9 on.

Montgomery, Rutherford G. *Carcajou;* il. by L. D. Cram. Caxton Printers, 1936. In describing the marauding career of that unpopular animal, the wolverine, the author gives at the same time a picture of the northern wilderness where wild beasts, Indians, and white trappers are engaged in a struggle for a livelihood. Ages 12–15.

Mukerji, Dhan Gopal. *Kari the Elephant;* il. by J. E. Allen. Dutton, 1922. This story of the growth and adventures of an elephant conveys potently the atmosphere of India. Ages 10–12.

Patch, Edith M. *Holiday Hill;* il. by Wilfrid S. Bronson. Macmillan, 1931. The other books by this author, *Holiday Meadow* and *Holiday Pond* and *Holiday Shore, Forest Neighbors,* and others which she has written in collaboration with Carroll Lane Fenton, are accurate and appealing. They make the life of American animals interesting and encourage firsthand observation. Ages 9–11.

Richards, Dick. *Life with Alice; Forty Years of Elephant Adventures.* Coward-McCann, 1944. The great friendship that grew up between Alice, the elephant, and Dick Richards, who was her keeper for forty years. Mr. Richards tells the story himself with humor and understanding. Ages 9–15 and on.

Robinson, Tom. *Mr. Red Squirrel;* il. by Kurt Wiese. Viking, 1943. This account of a friendship between a little girl and a wild squirrel of the woods, written with a genuine love of animals, shows a child how wild creatures can be tamed. Ages 7–9.

Salten, Felix. *Bambi;* il. by Kurt Wiese. Noble, 1935. The life story of a forest deer told simply and poetically. Ages 10–15.

Sanderson, Ivan T. *Animals Nobody Knows;* il. by the author. Viking, 1940. The author's lively style and brilliant drawings have resulted in a thrilling book telling about twenty-one strange and fascinating creatures which he drew from life in the jungles of Dutch Guiana. Ages 10–14.

Stearns, David M. *Chuckle: the Story of a Woodchuck;* il. by Sharon Stearns. Farrar, 1939. The life story of a woodchuck engagingly told and pictured. Ages 7–10.

Stevens, Alden G. *The Way of a Lion;* drawings by George Mason. Stokes, 1935. A graphic description of wild-animal life and habits. Ages 10–13.

Stong, Phil. *Honk: The Moose;* story by Phil Stong; pictures by Kurt Wiese. Dodd, 1935. Story and pictures tell with much humor what happens when two small boys in Minnesota discover a moose in the stable. Ages 8–10.

Waldeck, Jo Besse McElveen. *Little Lost Monkey;* pictures by Kurt Wiese. Viking, 1942. The story of a tiny Sakiwinki monkey who was separated from his mother and who roamed the New Guinea jungle till he found her. Told with a gentle humor and intimate knowledge of the country. Ages 7–10.

Waldeck, Theodore J. *Jamba the Elephant;* il. by Kurt Wiese. Viking, 1942. A fine story of a dangerous bull elephant and the young son of a skilled mahout whose patience and affection succeeded in turning Jamba into a useful carrier of ebony. The author is an explorer and well acquainted with the countries and animals of which he writes, in this and in his *Lions on the Hunt* (Viking, 1942) and *The White Panther* (Viking, 1941). Ages 10–14.

Waldeck, Theodore J. *Treks Across the Veldt;* il. by Ivan Sanderson. Viking, 1944. An account of an expedition to Tanganyika to bring back animals for zoos and laboratories. Full of excitement and suspense. Ages 9–15.

Wells, Rhea. *Zeke the Raccoon.* Viking, 1933. A friendly little story of a lovable, mischievous pet. Ages 5–9.

Wheeler, Post. *Hathoo of the Elephants.* Viking, 1943. The author, who knows India at firsthand, tells the story of a boy brought up by elephants, in a book that paints a vivid picture of the jungle and is full of fascinating elephant lore. Ages 10–12.

CHAPTER IX

The Circus

BEHIND the scenes at the circus is a topic perennially interesting to readers of all ages.

Bostock, Frank C. *Training of Wild Animals;* ed. by Ellen Velvin. Appleton-Century, 1903. The care and training of wild animals in captivity. Ages 9–15.

Bruce, Mary Grant. *Circus Ring.* Putnam, 1937. Lively, natural story of life in a traveling circus that visited small towns in Australia. Ages 9–12.

Clarke, John S. *Circus Parade;* il. from old prints and pictures, and modern photographs. Scribner, 1937. Ages 10–15.

Cooper, Courtney Ryley. *Lions 'n' Tigers 'n' Everything;* new ed. Little, 1936. Sidelights on the lives of animals in circuses and menageries. Ages 9–15.

Furbush, Lydia. *Circus Parade.* Macmillan, 1942. A panorama picture book for small children. Ages 5–7.

Moses, Horace S. *Here Comes the Circus;* il. by Susanne Suba. Houghton, 1941. Artist and author together have recaptured the joy of circus-going. Ages 7–10.

Smith, E. Boyd. *The Circus and All About It;* with sixteen il. in colors and twenty-nine in black and white by the author. Stokes, 1909. This artist has drawn the circus with beauty and imagination and an appreciation of the magic it holds for children. Ages 6–9.

CHAPTER X

Birds and Insects

Allen, A. A. *American Bird Biographies; Containing the Complete Life-Histories of Familiar Birds, Written in Autobiographical Form.* Comstock Pub. Co., 1934. Illustrated with ten color plates and ten wash drawings by George Miksch Sutton, and 190 photographs of the birds in nature by the author. Ages 10–15.

Boulton, Rudyerd. *Travelling with the Birds;* il. by W. A. Weber. Donohue, 1933. An authority on birds gives much interesting information about them in these chapters on bird migration. Ages 9–11.

Bronson, Wilfrid S. *Wonder World of Ants;* il. by the author. Harcourt, 1937. The lives of many types of ants described in interesting fashion and well illustrated in color and black and white. *The Grasshopper Book;* il. by the author. Harcourt, 1943. Information on grasshoppers and kindred insects, written with accuracy and enthusiasm. *Little Black Ant,* by Alice Crew Gall and Fleming Crew (Oxford, 1936), is enjoyed by younger children. Ages 9–12.

Cothren, Marion B. *Pigeon Heroes; Birds of War and Messengers of Peace.* Coward-McCann, 1944. The feats of famous pigeons from the time of Noah's Ark to the Second World War. Excellent photographs. Ages 10–15.

Curtis, Mary I. *From Robin to Junco; Stories of Birds and What They Do;* il. by Lemuel Palmer and Jerome Donovan; color photographs by Arthur A. Allen. Houghton, 1940. Twelve delightful color photographs, lively black and white drawings, and a readable text hold the attention of boys and girls, answer their questions, and stimulate observation. Ages 9–12.

DuBois, Theodora. *Banjo the Crow;* il. by Helen Torrey. Houghton, 1943. Amusing story of a pet crow. Ages 7–10.

Flack, Marjorie. *The Restless Robin.* Houghton, 1937. Tells accurately and with charm, in text and pictures, of the birds' spring migration. Ages 6–8.

Gaul, Albro T. *Picture Book of Insects;* il. with photographs by the author. Lothrop, 1943. Brief descriptions of twenty common insects, with full-page photographs that are sometimes beautiful and always interesting. A good "first book" on insects. Ages 8–12.

Kane, Henry B. *The Tale of the Crow;* il. by the author. Knopf, 1943. Remarkable photographs show every step in the development of a crow family. There are also delightful portraits of their forest neighbors. Ages 8–15.

Mathews, Schuyler. *Book of Birds for Young People;* with sixty-seven il. in color and twenty-eight in black and white by the author. Putnam, 1921. Frank M. Chapman's *Bird-Life; a Guide to the Study of Our Common Birds* (Appleton-Century, 1924) is still more comprehensive. *The Western Bird Guide,* by C. K. Reed (Doubleday, 1913), covers the birds of the Rockies and west to the Pacific. Ages 12–15.

Matschat, Cecile Hulse. *American Butterflies and Moths;* il. by Rudolf Freund. Random House, 1942. Good for identification, with accurate text and pleasing, authentic drawings in color and black and white. Ages 9–12.

Savage, Alma. *Eben the Crane;* il. by Charles Keller. Sheed and Ward, 1944. Eben is a bird with a droll personality. His life story, based on a true incident, is admirably recreated in this story of wild life in the Far North. Ages 9–12.

Teal, Edwin Way. *Near Horizons, the Story of an Insect Garden;* il. Dodd, 1942. Though written for adults, boys and girls interested in the subject will find the author's observations of insect life in an old Long Island orchard garden fascinating. His ability to describe insect habits makes this book absorbing reading. Younger readers interested in collecting will find the author's *The Boys' Book of Insects,* il. with photographs and drawings by the author (Dutton, 1939), very helpful. Ages 12–15.

CHAPTER XI

Snakes and Other Reptiles

Bronson, Wilfrid S. *Pollwiggle's Progress;* pictures and story by W. S. Bronson. Macmillan, 1932. Step by step in interesting, companionable fashion, with many drawings that are both enlightening and entertaining, the author describes for children the progress of a bullfrog through the various stages from frog's egg to pollywog to frog. The insect, plant, and animal life of pond and stream is made very vivid. Ages 8–10.

Bronson, Wilfrid S. *Turtles;* il. by the author. Harcourt, 1945. All the facts about turtles told with simplicity, humor, and accuracy, and illustrated with excellent drawings. Though planned for the younger children, older readers interested in turtles will enjoy it and find it useful. Ages 6–8.

Conant, Roger and Bridges, William. *What Snake Is That? A Field Guide to the Snakes of the United States East of the Rocky Mountains;* with 108 drawings by Edmonde Malnate. Appleton-Century, 1939. Makes identification easy. Ages 10–15.

Ditmars, Raymond Lee. *Book of Living Reptiles; Where the Crocodilians, Lizards, Snakes, Turtles and Tortoises Are Found;* il. by Helène Carter. Lippincott, 1936. Colored maps which locate various snakes, crocodiles, lizards, turtles, and tortoises in their native habitat, accompanied by brief descriptive text. Ages 10–14.

Eberle, Irmengarde. *Hop, Skip, and Fly; Stories of Small Creatures;* pictures by Else Bostelmann. Holiday House, 1937. Eight chapters about the young frog, the scorpion, bat, garter snake, and other creatures, written with exquisite clarity and illustrated with accuracy and charm. Ages 7–10.

Flack, Marjorie. *Tim Tadpole and the Great Bullfrog.* Doubleday, 1934. A picture book showing a tadpole's progress from
spring to midsummer. Brief, lively text and charming drawings.
Ages 4–8.

Pope, Clifford Hillhouse. *Snakes Alive, and How They Live;* il.
with photographs and including an illustrated key for the identification of the snakes of the United States. Viking, 1937. The
author's adventures while hunting and studying snakes in this
country and in China. Ages 12–15.

CHAPTER XII

Sea Life

Adshead, Gladys. *Casco;* pictures by Else Bostelmann. Oxford, 1943. A baby seal on the Maine coast who lost his mother before he was able to care for himself was saved from starvation by a kindly collie dog and his master. He became an interesting and affectionate pet before he swam away in the autumn to join his own kind. Based on fact, and well illustrated. Ages 7–10.

Bronson, Wilfrid S. *Children of the Sea;* il. by the author. Harcourt, 1940. The author describes, vividly, accurately, and with charm, dolphin life in northern and southern waters. The second half of the book tells the story of the friendship between the dolphin and Smudgy, a little boy of Nassau. Ages 10–14.

Bronson, Wilfrid S. *Fingerfins; the Tale of a Sargasso Fish;* pictures and story by W. S. Bronson. Macmillan, 1930. Scientifically accurate, this little book is written and illustrated with humor and imagination. Ages 8–10.

Bronson, Wilfrid S. *Paddlewings, the Penguin of Galápagos;* pictures by the author. Macmillan, 1931. Penguins are engaging creatures, and Paddlewings, as described by Mr. Bronson, is no exception to the rule. Ages 9–11.

Eberle, Irmengarde and Bostelmann, Else. *Sea-Horse Adventure;* il. by Else Bostelmann. Holiday House, 1937. Brief, accurate, and pleasantly told story of the life of a little sea-horse. Ages 8–11.

Huntington, Harriet E. *Let's Go to the Seashore;* il. with photographs by the author. Doubleday, 1941. An excellent first book for little children about the life of beach and shore, illustrated by the author's own photographs, which are not only beautiful, but clear and informing. Ages 6–8.

CHAPTER XIII

Trees and Flowers

House, Homer D. *Wild Flowers;* 364 full-color illustrations, with complete descriptive text. Macmillan, 1942. A wild flower identification book with remarkable color plates. Each plate is accompanied by a brief description and a note of the geographical range of the flower. Age 9 on.

Limbach, Russell T. *American Trees;* written and il. by Russell T. Limbach; with an introd. by T. H. Everett. Random House, 1942. Fifty-five different trees, the main types found in the U.S., are delightfully illustrated in color, with a clear, informative description of each tree, giving its characteristics and where it is to be found. Ages 9–12.

Lucas, Jannette May. *Fruits of the Earth;* with il. by Helène Carter. Lippincott, 1942. A history of the origins, the travels, and man's cultivation and development of his favorite fruits, with a simple explanation of their classification. Charming pictorial maps in soft colors. Ages 9–12. The author's *First the Flower, Then the Fruit,* il. by Helène Carter (Lippincott, 1943), continues the story by tracing the origin and development of the fig, date, grape, pomegranate, pineapple, and watermelon. Ages 10–14.

McKenny, Margaret. *A Book of Wayside Fruits;* il. by Edith F. Johnston. Macmillan, 1945. Here are all the berries of the wayside, edible or merely ornamental, with a descriptive text giving habitat and characteristics, and drawings in color which make this a beautiful book. By the same author and illustrator, *A Book of Wild Flowers* (Macmillan, 1929), and *A Book of Garden Flowers* (Macmillan, 1941). Age 9 on.

McKenny, Margaret. *Trees of the Countryside;* il. with lithographs by Alice Bird. Knopf, 1942. Descriptions of twenty-nine trees representative of different parts of this country, with twenty-nine full-page pictures in color showing each tree in its natural setting. Ages 10–12.

Maril, Lee. *Spice and Scent; Herbs in Fact and Fancy;* il. by the author. Coward-McCann, 1943. Authentic information and the charm, in both text and drawings, of the author's own affection for her subject. Also by this author, *Savor and Flavor; a Book About Wild Berries* (Coward-McCann, 1944), and *Crack and Crunch; Nuts in Fact and Fancy* (Coward-McCann, 1945). Age 9 on.

Mathews, Schuyler. *Book of Wild Flowers for Young People;* with thirty-two il. in color and 160 in black and white by the author. Putnam, 1923. Descriptions of the flowers as they appear from April to October, many illustrations, good index, and color charts. Ages 10–13.

Parsons, Mrs. Frances Theodora Dana. *How to Know the Wild Flowers;* il. by Marion Satterlee and A. L. Shaw; new ed. Scribner, 1921. Arranged according to color, this is an easy guide for boys and girls to use. Because it is written in a style with literary flavor and a background of poetry and legend, it is one of the most interesting of the flower books. Ages 10–15.

Webber, Irma E. *Travelers All.* W. R. Scott, 1944. The propagation of plants simply told, with illuminating pictures. Ages 4–5.

CHAPTER XIV

Folk Tales and Wonder Stories

A LOVE for fairy tales has its roots deep in human nature, and it is every child's right to enter the magic world of elves and pixies, enchanted princesses, giants and dragons and flying carpets. The folk tale and wonder story cultivate his imagination and deepen his sense of humor; they broaden his mental horizon and serve as a preparation for the appreciation of literature in later life.

FOLK TALES

Arabian Nights: Their Best-Known Tales; ed. by K. D. Wiggin and N. A. Smith; il. in color by Maxfield Parrish. Scribner, 1909. (Scribner's Illustrated Classics.) A treasure house of wonder and magnificence no child should miss. Other good editions are *Arabian Nights' Entertainments,* based on a translation from the Arabic by E. W. Lane, ed. for young people by F. J. Olcott, il. by M. S. Orr (Holt, 1913); and *Arabian Nights,* ed. by Padraic Colum, il. by Eric Papé (Macmillan, 1923, Children's Classics). Ages 9–12.

Asbjørnsen, Peter Christian. *East of the Sun and West of the Moon;* ed. and il. by Ingri and Edgar Parin d'Aulaire, adapted from the Dasent translation. Viking, 1938. Old tales from the Norwegian illustrated by these two artists with rare understanding and beauty. Mrs. Gudrun Thorne-Thomsen's *East o' the Sun and West o' the Moon and Other Norwegian Folk Tales,* il. by Frederick Richardson (Row, 1912), contains simpler versions. Ages 8–12.

Bowman, James C. and Bianco, Margery. *Tales from a Finnish Tupa;* from a translation by Aili Kolehmainen; pictures by Laura Bannon. Whitman, 1936. These stories have the tang of common sense, the wonder with which the folk tale invests all the homely, everyday things of life, and a sense of fundamental values. Ages 8–12.

Brenner, Anita. *The Boy Who Could Do Anything, and Other Mexican Folk Tales;* retold by Anita Brenner; il. by Jean Charlot. W. R. Scott, 1942. Twenty-four folk tales set down as they are being told in Mexico today. There is earthy vigor and humor in these stories, and Jean Charlot has illustrated them with originality and zest. Ages 8–12.

Brock, H. M., illustrator. *The Book of Fairy Tales.* Warne, 1928. Contains "Puss in Boots," "Jack and the Beanstalk," "Hop o' My Thumb," and "Beauty and the Beast," with pictures richly colored and full of the detail and characterization which children enjoy. Ages 6–10.

Brooke, L. Leslie. *The House in the Wood and Other Old Fairy Stories;* with drawings by L. Leslie Brooke. Warne, 1944. "The Brave Little Tailor," "The Bremen Town Musicians," "Snow-White and Rose-Red," and other old favorites illustrated with gaiety and humor. Ages 6–9.

Campbell, Alfred S. *The Wizard and His Magic Powder; Tales of the Channel Islands;* il. by Kurt Wiese. Knopf, 1945. Bits of folklore and legend showing how fairies and wizards and magic are accepted as a part of daily life in the islands. Ages 7–10.

Chan, Chih-Yi and Plato. *The Good-Luck Horse;* with a foreword by Carl Glick. Whittlesey House, 1943. The adaptation of an old Chinese legend, with unique and lovely drawings by a twelve-year-old Chinese boy. Ages 7–12.

Chase, Richard. *The Jack Tales;* told by R. M. Ward and his kindred in the Beech Mountain section of North Carolina and by other descendants of Council Harmon (1803–1896) elsewhere in the Southern Mountains; with three tales from Wise Co., Virginia; set down from these sources and edited by Richard Chase; with an appendix compiled by Herbert Halpert; and il. by Berkeley Williams, Jr. Houghton, 1943. Eighteen lively stories which the author heard told. We soon recognize Jack as our old friend who killed giants and climbed the beanstalk. The tales have freshness, humor, and a fine, colorful, American background. Ages 8–12.

Chrisman, Arthur Bowie. *Treasures Long Hidden: Old Tales and New Tales of the East;* il. by Weda Yap. Dutton, 1941. Chinese folk tales, retold for boys and girls, which have the age-old dignity and wisdom, the sense of justice and quiet humor of the great eastern land from which they come. Children should also know this author's *Shen of the Sea.* Dutton, 1925. Ages 9–12.

D'Aulaire, Ingri and Edgar Parin. *Don't Count Your Chicks.* Doubleday, 1943. A fine old folk tale which these artists have adorned with pictures of an enchanting gaiety that are thoroughly in the spirit of childhood. Ages 4–8.

De la Mare, Walter, comp. *Animal Stories;* chosen, arranged, and in some part rewritten by Walter de la Mare. Scribner, 1940. An anthology of animal tales taken chiefly from folklore. A valuable preface by Mr. de la Mare traces the development of the animal folk tale and comments on the stories. For pictures he has chosen quaint seventeenth-century woodcuts. Each story is preceded by a poem. Ages 9–12.

Carpenter, Frances. *Tales of a Swiss Grandmother;* il. by Ernest Biéler. Doubleday, 1940. Folk tales full of the mountain peaks, snowy ravines and avalanches, crops, cattle, and customs which are a part of the daily life of the Swiss people. Ernest Biéler's drawings catch completely the spirit of the tales. Another excellent collection of Swiss folk tales is *The Three Sneezes and Other Swiss Tales;* written and illustrated by Roger Duvoisin. Knopf, 1941. Ages 9–12.

Fenner, Phyllis R., comp. *Giants and Witches and a Dragon or Two;* stories selected by Phyllis R. Fenner. Knopf, 1943. Well-chosen folk tales of many lands, reprinted from other collections. Ages 8–11.

Fillmore, Parker H. *Czechoslovak Fairy Tales;* with il. and decorations by Jan Matulka. Harcourt, 1919. Mr. Fillmore has retold these tales with a fine appreciation of their fancy and humor. Ages 9–11.

Finger, Charles. *Tales from Silver Lands;* woodcuts by Paul Honoré. Doubleday, 1924. Nineteen legendary stories from South America, which the author heard at first hand. Mr. Finger has retold them with vigor, a sense of drama, and the flavor of the lands from which they come. Ages 10–13.

Galloway, Philippa. *Folk Tales from Scotland;* retold by Philippa Galloway and il. by Walter J. A. Cook. Collins, 1944. Tales which have the touch of strangeness and beauty characteristic of Celtic folklore. Ages 8–11.

Gillham, Charles Edward. *Beyond the Clapping Mountains; Eskimo Stories from Alaska;* il. by Chanimum. Macmillan, 1943. Tales which Eskimos of Alaska tell to one another of animals and water, kayaks, ice, snow, and hunting, and the wild geese flying north. They have a childlike humor and imagination. Remarkable illustrations by an Eskimo girl. Ages 8–12.

Grimm, J. L. K. and Grimm, W. K. *The House in the Wood and Other Old Fairy Stories;* with drawings by L. Leslie Brooke. Warne, 1910. Nine of the best-known stories, with delightful full-page pictures by an artist who knew how to draw for children. Other excellent editions are *Tales from Grimm,* freely trans. and il. by Wanda Gág; and *Household Stories,* trans. by Lucy Crane, il. by Walter Crane. Macmillan, 1926. (Children's Classics.) *Snow White and the Seven Dwarfs,* freely trans. and il. by Wanda Gág (Coward-McCann, 1938), is a fine, vigorous retelling; and the drawings for that and for her *Three Gay Tales from Grimm* (Coward-McCann, 1943), containing three of the less well-known tales, take the reader straight into the folklore world. Ages 8–9.

Haslip, Joan. *Fairy Tales from the Balkans;* retold by Joan Haslip. Collins, 1944. These tales from Yugoslavia have a rich vein of fantasy and a fine vigor. Ages 8–11.

Jacobs, Joseph, ed. *English Fairy Tales;* il. by J. D. Batten. Putnam, 1892. Includes "Tom Tit Tot," "The Three Sillies," "Old Woman and Her Pig," "Jack and the Beanstalk," "Jack the Giant Killer," "History of Tom Thumb," "Whittington and His Cat," and about fifty other tales. One of the most popular collections. Ages 9–12.

Kelsey, Alice Geer. *Once the Hodja;* il. by Frank Dobias. Longmans, 1943. Century-old folk tales from Turkey about Nasr-ed-
Din, the simple-minded country fellow whose talent for getting
himself into trouble was only exceeded by his ability to get himself out again. Good-natured fun with a background of shrewd
common sense. Ages 9–12.

Lang, Andrew, ed. *Blue Fairy Book;* il. by H. J. Ford and G. P. J.
Hood. Longmans, 1929. Also the *Green, Red, Brown,* and *Yellow Fairy Books* (Longmans). Tales from many different lands
collected by a man who thoroughly enjoyed the task.

Lim Sian-Tek. *Folk Tales from China;* with illustrations by William Arthur Smith. John Day, 1944. A careful selection of tales
from the great body of Chinese folk literature. Charmingly retold, and throwing light on the history of China. Age 12 on.

MacManus, Seumas, comp. *Donegal Fairy Stories.* Doubleday,
1900. Full of humorous exaggeration and turns of speech, these
retellings of Irish folk tales have the lilt of the spoken word.
The author's other collections, *In Chimney Corners* (Doubleday, 1899) and *Well o' the World's End* (Macmillan, 1929), are
also much enjoyed by older boys and girls. Ages 9–12.

Mason, Arthur. *The Wee Men of Ballywooden;* il. by Robert Lawson. Garden City Pub. Co., 1936. Humorous, vigorous tales of
"the little people," based on stories the author heard as a boy
in Ireland. Robert Lawson's imaginative drawings have a fine
originality and strength. The author's *From the Horn of the
Moon,* il. by Robert Lawson (Garden City Pub. Co., 1937), contains more stories of the same "wee men." Ages 8–12.

Pyle, Howard. *Wonder Clock; or, Four and Twenty Marvellous
Tales;* il. by the author. Harper, 1887. The salty humor, fancy,
and human nature in these tales, which are based on folklore,
delight boys and girls. *Pepper and Salt; or, Seasoning for Young
Folks* (Harper, 1887) is equally popular. Both are excellent for
reading aloud. Ages 7–12.

Rasmussen, Knud. *The Eagle's Gift; Alaska Eskimo Tales;* trans.
by Isobel Hutchinson; il. by Ernest Hansen. Doubleday, 1932.
There is strength, vigor, and poetry in these folk tales of the
North. Ages 10–13.

Rickard, J. A. *The Old Aztec Story Teller;* il. by William Brady. Ackerman, 1944. Tales of Old Mexico told in simple, friendly fashion with genuine atmosphere. Ages 8–12.

Sawyer, Ruth. *Picture Tales from Spain;* il. by Carlos Sanchez. Stokes, 1936. Tales which Ruth Sawyer heard in Spain retold in English with atmosphere and humor. Ages 4–12.

Steel, Mrs. Flora Annie, ed. *English Fairy Tales Retold;* il. by Arthur Rackham. Macmillan, 1918. (Children's Classics.) An excellent collection of forty of the best-loved of the English folk tales. Ages 4–11.

Watkins, Hope Brister. *The Cunning Fox and Other Tales;* il. by Henry Pitz. Knopf, 1943. Animal folk tales taken from a wide range of European sources and retold with dramatic quality and humor. Strong, humorous drawings by Henry Pitz. Ages 7–12.

Wu Ch'eng-En. *The Adventures of Monkey;* from the translation of Arthur Waley; pictures by Kurt Wiese. John Day, 1944. Seven chapters from the novel which set forth the cleverness and wit of Monkey, the famous hero of Chinese folklore. In *The Magic Monkey,* adapted from an old Chinese legend by Christine and Plato Chan, il. by Plato Chan (Whittlesey House, 1944), a Chinese girl and her brother, with humor and an engaging simplicity, retell for younger boys and girls the legend of how Monkey obtained his gift of magic. Plato Chan's drawings have vitality and a fine sense of space and motion. Ages 12–15.

Yeats, William Butler. *Irish Fairy and Folk Tales;* il. Modern Library. Rich collection of Irish folk material dealing with fairies, pookas, banshees, witches, charms, and spells. Yeats said, "I have tried to make it representative . . . of every kind of Irish folk faith." Ages 12–15.

Young, Ella. *The Unicorn with Silver Shoes;* il. by Robert Lawson. Longmans, 1932. Based on Irish folklore, these tales are full of beauty, wit, and wonder. In *The Wonder Smith and His Son,* il. by Boris Artzybasheff (Longmans, 1927), Miss Young retells fourteen legends of the mythical Gubbaun Saor (the Wonder Smith). Ages 9–15.

MODERN WONDER STORIES

Some of the best writing ever done for children is to be found among the modern fairy and wonder tales.

Alger, Leclaire. *Dougal's Wish;* il. by Marc Simont. Harper, 1943. How an old Scottish book and a wish made by a little boy of Scottish descent brought strange happenings to a farm in Pennsylvania. For a wild pony, discovered by the children, proved to be a Kelpie strayed from his home in Scotland. Ages 9–12.

Andersen, Hans Christian. *Fairy Tales;* trans. by Mrs. Edgar Lucas; il. by Charles, Thomas, and William Robinson. Dutton. Other good editions are *It's Perfectly True and Other Stories,* trans. by Paul Lyssac, il. by Richard Bennett (Harcourt, 1938); *Fairy Tales,* trans. by Jean Hersholt, il. by Fritz Kredel (The Heritage Press, 1944); and *Fairy Tales and Legends,* il. by Rex Whistler (Houghton, 1935). Andersen is not for the youngest readers, but every child, when he is ready, should become acquainted with the humor and wisdom and gentle satire of this great teller of tales. Ages 9–15.

Averill, Esther. *The Adventures of Jack Ninepins;* il. by the author. Harper, 1944. "Jack Ninepins" (who was different from all the other eight of the set) holds our interest from the time we meet him floating face down in Boston harbor. Aided by gulls, porpoises, and a whale, he manages to cross the Atlantic and reach the Seine, where he is fished out by a policeman and returned to his small owner. Told with imagination and quiet humor and delightfully illustrated. *The Cat Club; or, The Life and Times of Jenny Linsky,* by the same author (Harper, 1944), presents with a gay absurdity scenes from the life of black cat Jenny and her cat acquaintances in a child's spirit of make-believe. Ages 7–9.

Bacon, Josephine Daskam. *The Door in the Closet.* Viking, 1940. A story of the world "betwixt and between," for a door in a quite ordinary closet opens to let an imaginative little girl step out into one marvelous adventure after another. The mixture of reality and fancy is cleverly managed and the author writes with wit and humor and knowledge of human nature. Ages 9–12.

Bailey, Margery. *Whistle for Good Fortune; in Which It Is Shown How Six from Six Makes Six and One to Carry, with Other Riddles Here and There Along the Way;* il. by Alice B. Preston. Little, 1940. Modern stories written by an author so steeped in folk and fairy lore that they are akin in spirit to the old tales. Ages 8–11.

Baker, Margaret and Mary. *The Bakers' Big Book; an Omnibus of Stories and Pictures.* Dodd, 1941. Contains: "The Dog, the Brownie and the Bramble Patch"; "The Sad Princess"; "The Lost Merbaby"; "The Leprechaun"; "The Little Girl Who Curtsied"; "The Princess and the Beggar Maid." Some of the best-loved stories by this author and artist who manage to catch in their stories a fine folk flavor. Illustrated with delightful silhouettes that are a real part of the story. Ages 7–11.

Baker, Margaret and Mary. *Fifteen Tales for Lively Children;* il. by Mary Baker. Dodd, 1939. Fanciful short stories that have great variety and freshness. Children respond to their spontaneous fun and humor, and they are admirable for storytelling. Illustrated with silhouettes and line drawings. Ages 6–10.

Barrie, Sir James Matthew. *Peter and Wendy;* il. by F. D. Bedford. Scribner, 1911. For years Barrie's story has delighted children with its inimitable account of the adventures of Wendy and Michael and John when Peter Pan took them to the Never-Never Land to find there pirates and redskins and the Fairy, Tinker Bell. Ages 9–12.

Buchan, John. *Magic Walking-Stick;* il. by A. E. Becher. Houghton, 1932. An English schoolboy buys a walking-stick from a strange old man and thereafter, whenever he twirls the stick, is instantly whisked away into distant countries where strange adventure and magic are blended. Ages 9–12.

Bullett, Gerald W. *The Happy Mariners;* il. by C. Walter Hodges. Dodge, 1936. A combination of a fine sea story with magic and make-believe. Ages 9–12.

Burton, Earl and Linette. *The Exciting Adventures of Waldo;* il. by Helen Stone. Whittlesey House, McGraw-Hill, 1945. There is a fine outdoor flavor in this tale, and authors and artist have given real personality to Waldo, the little imperfectly made decoy duck, cast aside and lonely until he gains a friend in a little boy who finds him and keeps him as his favorite toy. Ages 6–9.

Carroll, Lewis. *Alice's Adventures in Wonderland; and Through the Looking-Glass;* il. by John Tenniel. Macmillan, 1923. 2 v. in 1. (Children's Classics.) A great book to be enjoyed from childhood to old age.

Carryl, Charles Edward. *Davy and the Goblin;* il. by E. B. Bensell and H. I. Bacharach. Houghton, 1928. (Riverside Bookshelf.) A humorously imaginative story that delights child and adult when shared. *The Admiral's Caravan* (Houghton, 1892) by this author also reads aloud well. Ages 8–11.

Casserley, Anne. *Michael of Ireland.* Harper, 1927. Imagination, humor, and engaging child and animal characters distinguish these Irish fairy tales. Ages 8–10.

Coatsworth, Elizabeth. *Knock at the Door;* il. by F. D. Bedford. Macmillan, 1931. How Stephen, who was born in Fairyland, rode forth to adventure in the world of men. The beauty of the story and its imaginative quality make the Fairy Hill seem very real. Ages 9–12.

Dunne, J. W. *St. George and the Witches;* il. by Lloyd Coe. Holt, 1939. The further adventures of St. George after he killed the dragon and, as a fitting sequel to this exploit, married the rescued princess. Mr. Dunne, with zest and humor, creates an amazing world that is both medieval and magical. Ages 9–12.

Farjeon, Eleanor. *Italian Peepshow and Other Tales;* il. by Rosalind Thorneycroft. Stokes, 1926. Gay little book about three English children living in Italy and the stories told them. Ages 8–10.

Farjeon, Eleanor. *Martin Pippin in the Apple Orchard.* Stokes, 1922. A fairy tale for older girls and adults, with a springtime quality of youth and gaiety and timelessness. *Martin Pippin in the Daisy Field* (Stokes, 1937) was written for somewhat younger readers. Ages 12–15.

Haldane, J. B. S. *My Friend Mr. Leakey;* il. by L. H. Rosoman; Harper, 1938. Mr. Leakey is a modern magician who in present-day London carries out his plans by means of a magic wand, a flying carpet, and his attendant Djinns. The book is written by a scientist with a careful attention to details and a solemn absurdity that is very funny. Ages 9–12.

Hoffmann, Eleanor. *Mischief in Fez;* il. by Fritz Eichenberg. Holiday House, 1943. Original, thrilling, and beautifully written tale of Djinns and magic in a Moroccan household. Details of native life in French North Africa are woven into this superb fantasy. Ages 9–12.

Jones, Elizabeth Orton. *Twig.* Macmillan, 1942. What happened in a city back yard when Twig, an imaginative little girl, made a little house for a fairy to live in out of a tomato can. Told with gaiety and humor. Ages 8–10.

Lang, Andrew. *Prince Prigio;* il. by Robert Lawson. Little, 1942. Children who have read many fairy tales and loved them will appreciate Andrew Lang's impish humor, faultless logic, and occasional gentle touch of satire. Mr. Lawson's lively, humorous drawings are completely in the spirit of this delightful tale. Ages 9–12.

Lawson, Marie A. *Dragon John;* il. by the author. Viking, 1943. A gay and charming tale of "a smallish dragon who was very lonely and most unhappy but who, in the end, came to a great and lasting joy." Ages 8–10.

Loring, Selden M. *Mighty Magic; an Almost True Story of Pirates and Indians;* pictures by Clara Skinner. Holiday House, 1937. When Jack Hollis went to visit his friend Granny Matten in her little house beyond Indian River, dusky Indians and black-bearded pirates stole out of the quiet woods, summoned by the magic of an old Indian drum; and in the events that followed, Jacky played his part in a story that belonged to the past and was also a part of the present. Ages 8–12.

Lowrey, Janet. *The Lavender Cat;* il. by Rafaello Busoni. Harper, 1944. A sensitive story lying between fantasy and reality; for the world which Jemmy, living among the Texas charcoal burners, created in his own imagination to escape from hardships, came true for him; and the little fairy cat, as he called her, led him to good fortune. Ages 9–12.

Macdonald, George. *At the Back of the North Wind;* il. by F. D. Bedford. Macmillan, 1924. (Children's Classics.) There is a rare and lovely quality in George Macdonald's fairy tales which brings a sense of spiritual values. *The Princess and the Goblin,* il. by F. D. Bedford (Macmillan, 1926); *The Princess and Curdie,* il. by Dorothy Lathrop (Macmillan, 1927); and *The Light Princess,* il. by Dorothy Lathrop (Macmillan, 1926), by this author are very popular and can be read by slightly younger children. Ages 10–12.

Masefield, John. *Midnight Folk.* Macmillan, 1927. An exciting, imaginative story that combines pirates, witches, black cats, magic, and a small boy's adventures. Ages 9–12.

Molesworth, Mrs. Mary Louisa. *The Cuckoo Clock; and The Tapestry Room;* il. by Walter Crane. Macmillan, 1925. (Children's Classics.) Two old-fashioned fairy tales which still charm. Ages 8–10.

Mulock, Dinah. *Adventures of a Brownie;* il. by E. E. Potter. Harper. When a family of children have a brownie for a playfellow, they must be prepared for surprises, but this particular brownie never did anyone harm unless he deserved it. Ages 7–10.

Mulock, Dinah. *Little Lame Prince;* il. by Hope Dunlap. Lippincott. First published in 1875. There is beauty and idealism in this tale of a prince and his magic traveling cloak. Ages 9–11.

Nesbit, E. *The Bastable Children;* containing "The Treasure Seekers," "The Would-Be-Goods," "The New Treasure Seekers"; pref. by Christopher Morley. Coward-McCann, 1928. This author writes with charm and humor and authority about real children who invariably manage to become part of a fairy tale. Her *Five Children* (Coward-McCann, 1930) contains the equally popular "Five Children and It," "The Phoenix and the Carpet," "Story of the Amulet." Ages 9–12.

Norton, Mary. *The Magic Bedknob; or, How to Become a Witch in Ten Easy Lessons;* il. by Waldo Pierce. Putnam, 1944. Original fantasy, genuine humor, and delightful, convincing children. Ages 9–12.

Parrish, Anne. *Floating Island;* il. by the author, with sketches by Mr. Doll. Harper, 1930. A story enjoyed by both children and adults for its rare combination of imagination, humor, and clever characterization. The author's drawings have the same beauty, humorous wisdom, and delicious absurdity as the text. Ages 9–11.

Richards, George. *The Fairy Dictionary.* Macmillan, 1932. A charming little book of fairy lore. Ages 8–10.

Ruskin, John. *King of the Golden River; or, The Black Brothers;* il. by Arthur Rackham. Lippincott, 1932. A spirited fairy tale with a satisfying moral, telling what happened to the cruel black brothers, to kindhearted little Gluck, and to Treasure Valley, their inheritance. Ages 8–11.

Saint Exupéry, Antoine de. *The Little Prince;* il. by the author; trans. from the French by Katharine Woods. Reynal, 1943. A mature, imaginative tale in which the author sets forth his feelings about the meaning of life. Age 9 on.

Sandburg, Carl. *Rootabaga Stories;* il. by Maud and Miska Petersham. Harcourt, 1936. 2 v. in 1. Stories told by a poet to his own children, full of poetry, nonsense, and philosophy. Ages 10–14.

Sauer, Julia. *Fog Magic;* with decorations by Lynd Ward. Viking, 1943. A deeply imaginative story in which a little girl moves between two worlds. Greta, who loves the fog, is a very real and human child of the present; the hundred-year-old village of Blue Cove, Nova Scotia, and its people, which she found in the heart of the fog, is an equally convincing bit of the past. Ages 9–12.

Tarn, William W. *Treasure of the Isle of Mist;* il. by Robert Lawson. Putnam, 1934. A lovely story with a deep current of human understanding. The setting is the Isle of Skye. Ages 11–14.

Thurber, James. *Many Moons;* il. by Louis Slobodkin. Harcourt, 1943. A charming modern fairy tale full of imagination, a gentle humor, and the wisdom of childhood. Ages 8–11.

Told under the Magic Umbrella; Modern Fanciful Stories for Young Children; sel. by the Literature Committee of the Association for Childhood Education; il. by Elizabeth Orton Jones.

Macmillan, 1939. An excellent anthology containing old favorites and others less well known. Elizabeth Orton Jones's illustrations add charm to the book. Ages 6–10.

Tolkien, J. R. R. *The Hobbit; or, There and Back Again;* il. by the author. Houghton, 1938. This describes a magnificent adventure that has to do with a dragon and his hoard and the dwarfs who claimed it. It is well written, filled with suspense, and seasoned with a quiet humor. Ages 9–12.

White, Eliza Orne. *Enchanted Mountain.* Houghton, 1911. A nonsense story with an underlying base of common sense. Ages 8–10.

CHAPTER XV

Myths

Benson, Sally. *Stories of the Gods and Heroes;* il. by Steele Savage. Dial Press, 1940. Based on Bulfinch's *Age of Fable* and skillfully edited without destroying the flavor of that famous work. Steele Savage's distinguished drawings have a power appropriate to the text. Ages 10–15.

Brown, Abbie Farwell. *In the Days of Giants; a Book of Norse Tales;* il. by E. B. Smith. Houghton, 1930. The Norse myths retold with humor and imagination. *The Children of Odin,* by Padraic Colum (Macmillan, 1920), carries the young reader along by its spirit of adventure and the poetry of its style. Ages 8–12.

Buckley, Elsie Finnimore. *Children of the Dawn; Old Tales of Greece;* il. by F. C. Papé. Stokes, 1908. These retellings of the stories of Eros and Psyche, Hero and Leander, Alcestis, Orpheus and Eurydice have great beauty. The author is thoroughly familiar with the original sources. Ages 12–14.

Hawthorne, Nathaniel. *The Wonder Book and Tanglewood Tales;* il. by Maxfield Parrish. Dodd, 1910. Hawthorne's retellings of the Greek mythological stories are little masterpieces of prose. Ages 9–10.

Kingsley, Charles. *The Heroes; or, Greek Fairy Tales.* Macmillan, 1936. Beautiful and dignified retellings of the stories of Perseus, the Argonauts, and Theseus. Ages 10–13.

Sellew, Catherine F. *Adventures with the Gods;* il. by George and Doris Hauman. Little, 1945. Sixteen stories of the gods and goddesses of Mt. Olympus and the heroes of Greek mythology, told very simply for younger children. Ages 6–10.

CHAPTER XVI

Legends and Hero Tales

THE great stories of the past, the legends of saints and warriors, poets and kings, are an important part of a child's literary inheritance. These epic tales have the qualities which boys and girls demand, simplicity of speech, singleness of motive, directness of action. They stretch and strengthen the imagination, suggest ideals, and provide the incentive to follow them. Some of the many fine retellings of great stories for young people are listed below.

Brown, Abbie Farwell. *Book of Saints and Friendly Beasts;* il. by Fanny Y. Cory. Houghton, 1900. Legends of the saints and the animals associated with them retold in simple style. Though not written for children, Helen Waddell's *Beasts and Saints,* woodcuts by Robert Gibbins (Holt, 1934), with its naïve accounts, taken from old chronicles, of friendships between men and animals delights many boys and girls. Ages 9–11.

Buck, Alån. *The Harper's Daughter;* il. by Richard Bennett. Oxford, 1940. This is a retelling of one of the world's most famous stories, the Irish legend of Deirdre, the daughter of the Chief Story Teller, or Harper, to Conchubar, King of Ulster. Alan Buck's spirited prose version is full of poetic feeling. He shows his familiarity with the Gaelic sources, and this story as he tells it has the easy transition from high and solemn beauty to the homely sayings and incidents of every day, characteristic of Gaelic literature. Ages 10–14.

Church, Alfred. *Iliad for Boys and Girls*. Macmillan, 1907. (Children's Classics.) *Odyssey for Boys and Girls*. Macmillan, 1925. (Children's Classics.) Simple, excellent retellings preserving the spirit of Homer. Padraic Colum in *The Children's Homer; the Adventures of Odysseus and the Tale of Troy* (Macmillan, 1925) has retold the Homeric stories in a vigorous and beautiful prose. Ages 8–12.

Colum, Padraic. *Legend of Saint Columba;* il. by Elizabeth Mac-Kinstry. Macmillan, 1935. The story of the warrior saint told against a background of poetry, scholarship, and the beauty of the Irish landscape. Ages 10–14.

Davis, Mary Gould. *Truce of the Wolf and Other Tales of Old Italy;* il. by Jay Van Everen. Harcourt, 1935. Seven Italian tales and legends retold for children. The first, "The Truce of the Wolf," is taken from *The Little Flowers of St. Francis*. Ages 9–11.

Farjeon, Eleanor. *Ten Saints;* il. by Helen Sewell. Oxford, 1936. The lives of St. Christopher, St. Martin, St. Bridget, St. Nicholas, St. Patrick, and others, told with beauty and sympathy. Ages 9–13.

Hosford, Dorothy. *The Sons of the Volsungs;* adapted from *Sigurd the Volsung,* by William Morris; il. by Frank Dobias. Macmillan, 1932. A fine retelling in rhythmic prose, of the story of Sigurd and Brynhild, based on William Morris's epic poem. Ages 12–15.

Hull, Eleanor. *The Boys' Cuchulain; Heroic Legends of Ireland;* sixteen il. in color by Stephen Reid. Crowell, 1910. The story of a great legendary hero of Ireland told for boys and girls with beauty and dignity. Ages 12–14.

Hyde, Martin Powell. *The Singing Sword; the Story of Sir Ogier the Dane;* il. by Philip Cheney. Little, 1930. The adventures of the young son of the Duke of Denmark, left at the Court of Charlemagne as hostage for the good conduct of his father, makes a stirring tale. Ages 11–13.

Irving, Washington. *Legends of the Alhambra;* ed. by Mabel Williams; il. by Warwick Goble. Macmillan, 1926. (Children's Classics.) Irving brings to his readers the enchantment of the Alhambra's towers, courts, fountains, and rose gardens; its mysterious princesses, Arabian astrologers, talking ravens, and buried treasure. Ages 11–15.

Jagendorf, Moritz Adolf. *Tyll Ulenspiegel's Merry Pranks;* il. by Fritz Eichenberg. Vanguard, 1938. In retelling them, Mr. Jagendorf emphasizes the perennial youth and gaiety of these tales of the most nimble-witted rascal known to legend and tradition. Delightfully humorous illustrations. *Eleven Merry Pranks of Till the Jester;* freely narrated by Erich Kästner (Longmans, 1938), can be read by younger children. It has ten fine illustrations in color and many drawings by Walter Trier full of the spirit of the Middle Ages. Ages 9–13.

Pyle, Howard. *The Merry Adventures of Robin Hood;* il. by the author. Scribner, 1933. The best of all versions for boys and girls of the Robin Hood tales and a classic in itself. Ages 9–13.

Pyle, Howard. *The Story of King Arthur and His Knights;* il. by the author. Scribner, 1933. The author's imagination, his deep interest in medieval romances, and a background of wide reading make this one of the most alive and convincing versions of the stories of King Arthur. Followed by *The Story of the Champions of the Round Table* (Scribner, 1905); *The Story of Launcelot* (Scribner, 1907); *The Story of the Grail and the Passing of Arthur* (Scribner, 1910). For each one, Mr. Pyle made pictures which are completely a part of the story. Ages 10–13.

Seredy, Kate. *The White Stag;* il. by the author. Viking, 1937. Miss Seredy's magnificent drawings are an integral part of her spirited retelling of the epic of the Hun-Magyar migration. Ages 10–14.

Song of Roland. *Roland the Warrior;* by Virginia M. Collier and Jeanette Eaton; il. by F. E. Schoonover. Harcourt, 1934. The authors have combined fact and legend about Charlemagne and his knights. *The Song of Roland,* by Merriam Sherwood (Longmans, 1938), is an admirable translation for young people, made with scholarship and spirit. Ages 10–14.

Stephens, James. *Irish Fairy Tales;* il. by Arthur Rackham. Macmillan, 1920. The legends of Fionn, leader of the Fianna and father of Oisin, retold with beauty and humor by a poet. Ages 10–14.

CHAPTER XVII

History

"History," wrote Hendrik Van Loon in the foreword to his *History of Mankind*, "is the mighty Tower of Experience, which Time has built amidst the endless fields of bygone ages. It is no easy task to reach the top of this ancient structure and get the benefit of the full view. There is no elevator, but young feet are strong and it can be done."

Baity, Elizabeth Chesley. *Man Is a Weaver;* il. with photographs, and with drawings and maps by C. B. Falls. Viking, 1942. The long story of cloth, and how, through the centuries, man has made it; how he has spun it, woven it and dyed it, fashioned it into clothing for himself, and used it for many another purpose. The author follows one thread, man's accomplishment in the making of cloth, but shows it to be a part of a greater whole, so that her book is not only a historical account of textiles but a history of mankind through the ages. A wealth of illustrations and maps adds to the book's usefulness. Ages 10–13.

Farjeon, Eleanor. *Mighty Men from Achilles to Julius Caesar;* il. by Hugh Chesterman. Appleton-Century, 1925. *Mighty Men from Beowulf to William the Conqueror,* il. by Hugh Chesterman (Appleton-Century, 1925), are well-written stories of heroes of history and legend that are good to read aloud. Ages 8–11.

Hartman, Gertrude. *The World We Live In and How It Came to Be.* Macmillan, 1931. The author emphasizes beginnings, basic facts from which great movements have developed. There are more than 300 illustrations from contemporary sources. Ages 10–14.

Hibben, Thomas. *The Carpenter's Tool Chest;* il. by the author. Lippincott, 1933. An unusual little book, well illustrated, which describes today's tools and their uses and gives a clear account of tools through the ages, emphasizing the relation of the carpenter and his tools to important events in history. Ages 9–13.

Hillyer, Virgil M. *Child's History of the World;* il. by C. M. Boog and M. S. Wright. Appleton-Century, 1924. A continuous narrative, in simple conversational style, of what has happened from prehistoric times to the present, told by epochs and not by nations. Ages 9–12.

Parsons, Geoffrey. *Stream of History;* decorations by James Daugherty. New rev. ed. Scribner, 1933. A survey of the world in successive ages from prehistoric times to the present. Ages 12–15.

Seeger, Elizabeth. *Pageant of Chinese History;* il. by B. C. Watkins. Longmans, 1934. A well-written, interesting history of China for boys and girls. Ages 11–14.

Van Loon, Hendrik Willem. *Story of Mankind.* Garden City Pub. Co., 1931. The story of the human race told dramatically, picturesquely, and lighted with humor. Mr. Van Loon's spirited drawings and maps add to the charm of the book. Ages 11–14.

CHAPTER XVIII

Prehistoric Times

Adshead, Gladys L. *Something Surprising;* pictures by Helen Rinald. Oxford, 1939. The first signs of life on this planet and the great creatures of long ago described in a way that is clear, interesting, and within the reading ability of the younger children. Excellent drawings. Ages 8–10.

Ditmars, Raymond Lee. *The Book of Prehistoric Animals;* picture maps by Helène Carter. Lippincott, 1935. Interesting text supplemented by maps in color showing where the extinct creatures of the past came from. Ages 10–13.

Fenton, Carroll Lane. *Life Long Ago; the Story of Fossils.* Day, 1937. The story of plant and animal life written in stone to be discovered after millions of years. Ages 10–15.

Knight, Charles Robert. *Before the Dawn of History.* McGraw, 1935. Reproductions of the forty-four panoramic paintings of prehistoric animals which the author prepared for natural history museums in the United States, with descriptions of the life of these strange creatures. Ages 10–14.

Perkins, Lucy Fitch. *The Cave Twins.* Houghton, 1916. The story for young children of a little brother and sister of prehistoric times. Ages 7–8.

Robinson, William Wilcox. *Ancient Animals;* il. by Irene B. Robinson. Macmillan, 1934. Information about prehistoric life and the mighty animals that once inhabited our continent. The illustrations are vigorous and graphic. Ages 10–13.

Smith, E. Boyd. *So Long Ago;* il. by the author. Houghton, 1944. These pictures, with their exquisite coloring, their gaiety, and humor, are likely to arouse in seven- and nine-year-olds an affectionate interest in the great, extraordinary creatures who once inhabited our globe. Age 7 on.

Williams, Henry Lionel. *Turi of the Magic Fingers;* with fifty-two drawings by Harry Daugherty. Viking, 1939. Satisfying, convincing story of early man. Ages 8–11.

CHAPTER XIX

Ancient Civilizations

Hall, Jennie. *Buried Cities;* with many drawings and photographs from original sources. Macmillan, 1922. Miss Hall describes the early life and excavations of Pompeii, Olympia, and Mycenae. Fine photographs. Ages 9–13.

Mayer, Josephine and Prideaux, Tom, eds. *Never to Die: The Egyptians in Their Own Words;* sel. and arr. with commentary. Viking, 1938. Splendid presentation of the Egypt of 3000 years ago. A book for boys and girls and readers of any age. Ages 12–15.

Means, Philip. *Tupak of the Incas;* by Philip Means, with editorial assistance from Alice Dalgliesh; il. by H. M. Herget. Scribner, 1942. An authority on Peruvian history and archaeology has written a story describing the life in the Inca kingdom before the Spanish conquest. Full of accurate details. Ages 10–12.

White, Anne Terry. *Lost Worlds: Adventures in Archaeology.* Random House, 1941. How men have sought and found the records of four great civilizations; Crete, Egypt, Babylonia-Assyria, and the Mayan of Central America. An admirable introduction to the science of archaeology. Fine photographs. Ages 12–16.

CHAPTER XX

The Middle Ages

Boutet de Monvel, M. *Joan of Arc*. Appleton-Century, 1907. A beautiful picture book which preserves the spirit of fifteenth-century France in its pages. Ages 9–13.

Chute, Marchette. *The Innocent Wayfaring;* decorations by the author. Scribner, 1943. Romance, humor, and human nature are in this light-hearted story of youth and first love in Chaucer's England. Ages 12–15.

Davis, William Stearns. *Life on a Medieval Barony*. Harper, 1922. Description of a typical medieval seigniory in Northern France in the year 1220. Ages 12–15.

French, Allen. *The Lost Baron; a Story of England in the Year 1200;* with il. by Andrew Wyeth. Houghton, 1940. A good picture of medieval life, with a spice of mystery. Ages 11–14.

Gray, Elizabeth Janet. *Adam of the Road;* il. by Robert Lawson. Viking, 1942. A picture of thirteenth-century England, thoroughly authentic and made extraordinarily real by the author's power to imagine the past deeply and sensitively. Splendid drawings by Robert Lawson show the medieval countryside, castles, towers, inns, and wayfarers. Ages 10–14.

Lamprey, Louise. *In the Days of the Guild;* il. by Florence Gardiner and Mabel Hatt. Stokes, 1918. Charming stories, each one centering on the beginning of some guild industry. Also, *Masters of the Guild* (Stokes, 1920) by the same author. Ages 10–14.

Leighton, Margaret. *Twelve Bright Trumpets;* il. by Frank Dobias. Houghton, 1942. Twelve well-written stories about adventures and everyday life of boys and girls in the Middle Ages. Each story is based on a stirring event or a vital turning point in European history. Ages 11–14.

Rosenberg, Melrich. *The Ark of Heraldry;* decorations by Elinore
Blaisdell. Holt, 1939. Short accounts of fifty-three heraldic crea-
tures, real and imaginary, which the knights and nobles of the
Middle Ages used on their shields and emblems. Ages 12–14.

Tappan, Eva March. *When Knights Were Bold.* Houghton, 1911.
A picture of life in castles, manors, monasteries, and towns during the Middle Ages. The descriptions of knightly customs are
given in detail. Ages 10–14.

CHAPTER XXI

The Days of the Discoverers

Averill, Esther. *Voyages of Jacques Cartier;* retold by Esther Averill; il. by Feodor Rojankovsky. Viking, 1937. The author has used liberal quotations from Cartier's own narrative. Fine pictures. Ages 11–13.

D'Aulaire, Ingri and Edgar Parin. *The Conquest of the Atlantic.* Viking, 1933. The illustrations, which are an integral part of the narrative, express the spirit of adventure, the courage and curiosity of the early voyagers. Ages 10–12.

Duvoisin, Roger. *They Put Out to Sea; the Story of the Map;* il. by the author. Knopf, 1944. The most memorable voyages from those of the Phoenicians, Cretans, and early Greeks to Magellan's journey round the world. A readable, vivid text, with many pictures. Ages 9–12.

Hewes, Agnes Danforth. *Spice Ho! A Story of Discovery;* drawings by Wilfred Jones. Knopf, 1941. A non-fictional account of the part played by the spice trade in the history of the world. Ages 10–14.

Kent, Louise Andrews. *He Went with Magellan;* il. by Paul Quinn. Houghton, 1943. The story of Magellan's perilous voyage around the world as seen through the eyes of a fourteen-year-old Portuguese boy. Ages 11–14.

Lucas, Mary Seymour. *Vast Horizons;* il. and maps by C. B. Falls. Viking, 1943. Panoramic story of discovery over four and a half centuries of time, carefully related to the history of the countries concerned. The author includes unusual source material, and portraits of individuals are drawn with skill and sympathy. Fine maps showing the world in different centuries, trade routes, and the routes of explorers. Ages 11–14.

Outhwaite, Leonard. *Unrolling the Map: The Story of Exploration;* with drawings of ships by Gordon Grant, and fifty-six specially devised maps; rev. ed. Day, 1938. The history of exploration from 3000 B.C. to the present. Ages 12–14.

Sondergaard, Arensa. *My First Geography of the Pacific;* il. by Cornelis. Little, 1944. Well-written, simple accounts of Balboa, Magellan, and other early adventurers, and an explanation of the importance of the islands of the Pacific in the recent war. Beautiful pictures in bright colors help answer the questions of young readers. Ages 7–10.

Sondergaard, Arensa. *They Went Exploring;* il. by C. H. DeWitt. Harper, 1942. In simple, charming prose the author tells of the explorers from the days of the Phoenicians down to the present. Many illustrations in color. Ages 7–10.

Synge, Margaret Bertha. *A Book of Discovery, the History of the World's Exploration from the Earliest Times to the Finding of the South Pole.* Putnam, 1912. This fascinating account of explorations everywhere and at all periods in history owes much of its charm to the fact that many of the explorers tell part of their own story in their own words, and also to a generous use of the reproductions of old maps and contemporary woodcuts. Ages 11–14.

CHAPTER XXII

England

Brown, Beatrice Curtis and Arbuthnot, Helen. *The Story of England;* il. by Gustaf Tenggren. Random House, 1943. Many fine, full-page pictures in color, and a simple, direct telling of England's story with emphasis on dramatic events and picturesque characters. Ages 8–10.

Gibson, Katharine. *Bow Bells;* il. by Vera Bock. Longmans, 1943. The author expands the legend in a fashion to make old London, the Bow Church bells, and Dick Whittington, the country boy who came to London to seek his fortune, very real. Ages 9–12.

Quennell, Marjorie and C. H. B., *History of Everyday Things in England.* 4 v. in 3. Scribner, 1918–35. A storehouse of information on all aspects of life in England from 1066–1934. Profusely illustrated with drawings, plans, colored plates, and photographs. Ages 12–15.

Williams-Ellis, Amabel Strachey and Fisher, F. J. *The Story of English Life;* il. by Wilma Hickson. Coward-McCann, 1936. A social history of England, illustrated with delightful charts and sketches. Ages 11–14.

Wilson, J. Dover. *Through Elizabethan Eyes;* an abridgment of *Life in Shakespeare's England,* for junior readers. Macmillan, 1939. A delightful little book which a distinguished Shakespearean scholar has abridged from his own larger work. Illustrated by reproductions of contemporary prints. Ages 12–15.

CHAPTER XXIII

The Continent of Europe

Kelly, Eric P. *The Land of the Polish People;* il. from photographs. Lippincott, 1944. (Portraits of the Nations, a Series for Young People.) An excellent book written with a knowledge of Poland, past and present, admiration and affection for the Polish people, and familiarity with that country's rich store of legend and tradition. Fine photographs. Other titles in this excellent series are *The Land of William of Orange,* by A. J. Barnouw; *The Land of the Russian People,* by Alexander Nazaroff; *The Land of the Chinese People,* by Cornelia Spencer. Ages 9–14.

White, William C. *Made in USSR;* il. with photographs. Knopf, 1944. An enlarged edition of an earlier book, describing the arts and handicrafts of Soviet Russia and in so doing telling much about folklore, geography, history, and social conditions. Ages 11–15.

CHAPTER XXIV

North America

Adams, Randolph. *Gateway to American History*. Little, 1927. The period of exploration and first settlements in America described in easy, conversational style. Many valuable contemporary pictures are reproduced. Ages 11–14.

Holling, Holling Clancy. *Paddle-to-the-Sea;* written and il. by Holling Clancy Holling. Houghton, 1941. An Indian boy carves a little figure in a canoe a foot long and starts it on a journey through the different waterways, across the Great Lakes, and down the St. Lawrence to the ocean. Geography presented with freshness, originality, and imagination. Ages 7–11.

Kenton, Edna. *With Hearts Courageous;* il. by Raphael Doktor. Liveright, 1933. A book which gains force and vividness because the author has followed closely the original accounts kept by the Jesuit missionaries who came to America in the seventeenth century. Ages 12–15.

Peck, Anne Merriman and Johnson, Enid. *Roundabout America;* il. by A. M. Peck. 2 v. Harper, 1933. Interesting, informative travel narrative which begins with a glimpse of Washington and ends with a trip by water from San Francisco to New York. Ages 11–14.

Skinner, Constance Lindsay. *Beaver, Kings and Cabins;* with il. by W. Langdon Kihn. Macmillan, 1933. The story of the early French and English fur traders vividly told. Ages 12–14.

CHAPTER XXV

Canada

Boswell, Hazel. *French Canada;* pictures by the author. Viking, 1938. The artist-author has given her book, which tells of fact and legend in Quebec, an unusual quality by following in her pictures the type of drawing and design used by French Canadian women for their hooked rugs. The result is fresh and delightful. Ages 9–13.

Bonner, Mary Graham. *Canada and Her Story.* Knopf, 1942. Presents in readable fashion the history, geography, everyday life, people, and wild life of Canada. The author's *Made in Canada* (Knopf, 1943) describes Canadian arts and handicrafts and is illustrated by many photographs. Ages 12–15.

Peck, Anne Merriman. *Young Canada;* il. by the author. McBride, 1943. Describes in interesting fashion the life and background of the young people of Canada today. Ages 12–15.

CHAPTER XXVI

Mexico

Herzog, B. G. *Cortez and the Conquest of Mexico by the Spaniards in 1521; Being the Eyewitness Narrative of Bernal Diaz del Castillo, Soldier of Fortune and Conquistador with Cortez in Mexico;* abridged and edited by B. G. Herzog and il. with sixteenth-century Indian drawings of the conquest. W. R. Scott, 1942. Contemporary account of the Spanish conquest of Mexico, admirably edited for young readers from the translations of Maudsley, Keating, and Lockhart. The direct style makes this narrative very satisfying to boys and girls, and the contemporary drawings add interest. Ages 11–15.

Lansing, Marion. *Liberators and Heroes of Mexico and Central America;* il. from photographs. Page, 1941. The struggle for independence in Mexico and Central America outlined in sketches of the men who played a leading part. Ages 12–15.

Prescott, William H. *The Conquest of Mexico;* with il. by Keith Henderson and an introd. by Carl Van Doren. Doubleday, 1934. Prescott's long work brought within readable limits for boys and girls by eliminating the first part on Aztec civilization and the third part on the later life of Cortez. Keith Henderson's beautiful illustrations and decorations made from Aztec designs enhance the vividness of the narrative. Ages 13–15.

Smith, Susan Cowles. *Made in Mexico;* il. by Julia Castellanos. Knopf, 1930. This little book on decoration and handicraft in Mexico today, sheds light on the daily life of the people. Ages 10–14.

CHAPTER XXVII

America Past and Present

Averill, Esther. *Daniel Boone;* il. by Feodor Rojankovsky. Harper, 1945. The story of Daniel Boone told in many remarkable lithographs in color and in a text so imaginative and splendidly simple that it will appeal to readers of a wide range in age. Age 7 on.

Baer, Marian E. *Pandora's Box: The Story of Conservation;* il. by Allen Pope, Jr. Farrar, 1939. A readable, accurate book on a vital subject. Ages 11–14.

Bailey, Carolyn Sherwin. *Pioneer Art in America;* with lithographs by Grace Paull. Viking, 1944. American artists and their crafts shown in relation to the periods in which they lived. This, with the author's *Children of the Handcrafts; Tops and Whistles; Homespun Playdays* (Viking, 1935–41), gives much authentic information on the development of arts and crafts in America. Ages 10–12.

Barksdale, Lena. *That Country Called Virginia;* with lithographs by Grace Paull. Knopf, 1945. The author has used recent historical findings that cover the origin and early development of this state, and she writes with charm and humor as well as historical perspective. Ages 10–15.

Becker, May Lamberton, ed. *Growing Up with America: An Anthology.* Stokes, 1941. A well-chosen anthology which begins with tales of colonial times and ends with stories of the present day. Ages 11–14.

Benét, Rosemary Carr and Stephen Vincent. *Book of Americans;* il. by Charles Child. Farrar, 1933. Fifty-six poems in meters that are lively and varied, dealing with the lives and characters of famous men and women from Columbus to Woodrow Wilson. Ages 9–13.

DeWitt, C. H. *The Story of New England;* lithographs by C. H. DeWitt; text by Marshall McClintock. Harper, 1941. Simple text with eighteen full-page spirited lithographs and many black and white drawings. Other attractive volumes in Mr. DeWitt's excellent series of pictorial geographies about American regions are *The Story of the Pennsylvania Dutch,* lithographs by C. H. DeWitt, text by Ann Hark (Harper, 1943); *The Story of the Great Plains,* lithographs by C. H. DeWitt (Harper, 1943); and *The Story of California,* lithographs by C. H. DeWitt (Harper, 1944). Ages 9–12.

Emerson, Caroline D. *Old New York for Young New Yorkers;* il. by Alida Conover. Dutton, 1932. Miss Emerson has pictured episodes in the history of New York, from the days of the Indians until 1898, in a way to help young readers see the relation between past and present. Ages 9–12.

Foster, Genevieve. *George Washington's World;* il. by the author. Scribner, 1941. Selecting the years spanned by the life of George Washington and using him as the central point, the author has brought into relation the outstanding personalities and events which shaped the course of the years. In this attempt to correlate world events at a given period of history, the author has been brilliantly successful. Her *Abraham Lincoln's World,* il. by the author (Scribner, 1944), is equally successful. Ages 10–15.

Hartman, Gertrude. *These United States, and How They Came to Be.* Macmillan, 1935. The growth of this country from the time before the white men came, to the First World War, with emphasis on discoveries and inventions. Hundreds of old prints and engravings and many illustrations from rare books supplement the text. Ages 9–14.

Holland, Rupert Sargent. *Freedom's Flag; the Story of Francis Scott Key.* Macrae-Smith, 1943. The life of an American patriot and brilliant lawyer who lived between the American Revolution and the Civil War. Includes a description of the historic night which Francis Scott Key spent in the hands of the British, watching the attack on Fort Henry while the words of the Star-Spangled Banner took shape in his mind. Ages 12–15.

Huberman, Leo. *We, the People;* il. by T. H. Benton. Harper, 1932. A history for young people written from the social and economic standpoint. Ages 12–14.

Irving, Washington. *Knickerbocker's History of New York;* ed. by Anne Carroll Moore; il. by James Daugherty. Doubleday, 1928. Miss Moore's wise deletion of several thousand words and James Daugherty's vigorous drawings will help boys and girls to discover the lively fun, solemn absurdity, and stirring incidents of Irving's masterpiece. Ages 12–15.

Lawson, Robert. *Watchwords of Liberty; a Pageant of American Quotations;* selected and illustrated by Robert Lawson. Little, 1943. More than fifty of the famous quotations which are associated with memorable moments in our history, from colonial days to the third year of the Second World War, with stirring drawings. Ages 8–15.

Reed, W. Maxwell. *America's Treasure;* ed. by Carey Croneis; il. with photographs. Harcourt, 1939. The author discusses the world importance of America's natural resources; notes her extensive deposits of iron, coal, petroleum, and precious metals; explains the methods of extracting them; and emphasizes the need for conservation. Ages 12–15.

Sondergaard, Arensa. *A History of the United States for Young People;* il. by Cornelis. Random House, 1941. In simple prose the author has put the history of this country into a form which can be read and enjoyed by the younger boys and girls. The pictures, in color, which appear on every page, enhance the interest of the text. Ages 7–10.

CHAPTER XXVIII

Indians

Clark, Ann Nolan. *Little Navajo Bluebird;* il. by Paul Lantz. Viking, 1943. This beautiful, distinguished story of a little Indian girl and her family will start young readers on the road to intelligent sympathy with their fellow Americans in the Southwest. Ages 9–12.

Gale, Elizabeth. *The Winged Boat;* il. by Hervé Stein. Putnam, 1942. A story of the Manhattan Indians in the days when the Half Moon sailed up the Hudson River. Based on history, the book has authentic background and an interesting plot. Ages 9–12.

Lenski, Lois. *Indian Captive; the Story of Mary Jemison;* written and il. by Lois Lenski. Stokes, 1941. The story of the first two years which Molly Jemison, the white girl carried off by Seneca Indians, spent with her captors. Indian life is presented with accuracy and fine detail, and the heroine emerges as a real and appealing personality. Ages 9–12.

Salomon, Julian H. *The Book of Indian Crafts and Indian Lore;* with many il. by the author and others. Harper, 1928. Much useful material on Indian customs, dances, ceremonies, costumes, and directions for staging a pageant. Ages 11–14.

Schevill, Margaret Erwin. *In the Garden of the Home God; a Retelling of a Navajo Tale;* plates by Louise Ewing after the drawings by the author. Santa Fe Press, 1943. A story of planting and harvest, threaded with Indian songs. The beautiful illustrations are adapted from Navajo sand paintings. Age 9 on.

Schultz, James W. *Sinopah, the Indian Boy;* with il. by E. Boyd
Smith. Houghton, 1913. The true story of a Blackfoot Indian
boy, son of a chief. His later adventures are told in *With the
Indians in the Rockies.* Houghton, 1925. The author, who has
written many other stories about the Indians, lived for many
years with the Blackfoot tribe. Ages 9–13.

Sperry, Armstrong. *Little Eagle, a Navajo Boy;* written and il. by
Armstrong Sperry. Winston, 1938. The story of a fourteen-year-
old Navajo boy in the Cañon de Chelley, Arizona, where he
tends sheep, learns to work in silver, tracks down his sister's pony
which is stolen by a Ute Indian chief, and finally attains his
ambition to go to the government school. Ages 8–9.

Verrill, A. Hyatt. *Our Indians; the Story of the Indians of the
United States.* Putnam, 1935. A history of the Indian tribes of
the United States, their customs, habits, costumes, houses, occupations, and religions. Ages 10–14.

CHAPTER XXIX

Early Days in the Colonies

Barksdale, Lena. *The First Thanksgiving;* il. by Lois Lenski. Knopf, 1942. When Hannah spends Thanksgiving Day with her grandparents and relatives, she hears her grandmother's story of the first Thanksgiving feast at Plymouth, at which she and Grandfather were present. Told as the story of one who was there, the First Thanksgiving is made unusually vivid. Pleasing, lively drawings. Ages 8–10.

Berry, Erick. *Hudson Frontier;* pictures by the author. Oxford, 1942. A story of Albany in 1664 when it was a prosperous frontier city. It gives a lively authentic picture of the life of the young people of the town, and tells how some of them succeeded in solving a mystery. Ages 11–12.

Bradford, William, and others of the Mayflower Company. *Homes in the Wilderness; a Pilgrim's Journal of Plymouth Plantation in 1620, by William Bradford and Others of the Mayflower Company;* il. with drawings by Mary Wilson Stewart. W. R. Scott, 1939. First published in London in 1622 as *A Relation or Journal of the Plantation Settled in Plymouth in New England.* In this edition the language has been somewhat modernized but the flavor of the original, vigorous King James English has been preserved. The sturdy, direct narrative, with its details of the settlers' experiences, pleases boys and girls. Ages 10–13.

Field, Rachel Lyman. *Calico Bush;* il. by Allan Lewis. Macmillan, 1931. The hardships of pioneer life and the danger from hostile Indians are made very vivid in this story of colonial Maine in the days of its first settlement. Ages 12–14.

Follett, Helen. *House Afire!;* with il. by Armstrong Sperry. Scribner, 1941. A lively, natural, and authentic story of New York in the days when Governor Stuyvesant's leather-bucket brigade provided a remedy for the constant loss of property by fire. Helped by Mr. Sperry's fine drawings with their humor and liveliness, the book seems to set in motion the whole life of the town. Ages 8–10.

Lenski, Lois. *Puritan Adventure;* il. by the author. Lippincott, 1944. Interesting, very human story of the Massachusetts Bay Colony, well-drawn characters and many authentic details of Puritan life. Ages 9–12.

Woodward, Hildegarde. *Jared's Blessing.* Scribner, 1942. An appealing story of the little son of a minister in pre-Revolutionary Connecticut, and his mischievous puppy, inappropriately named Blessing. Miss Woodward writes with imaginative understanding, and her story and fine pictures convey a real feeling of life in colonial New England. Ages 8–10.

CHAPTER XXX

Cowboys and the West

Driggs, Howard R. *The Pony Express Goes Through; an American Saga Told by Its Heroes;* il. in color and black and white by William H. Jackson. Stokes, 1935. True stories told to the author by the riders and station agents of the Pony Express. The artist knew the West in Pony Express days. Ages 10–14.

Holling, Holling Clancy. *The Tree in the Trail;* written and il. by Holling Clancy Holling. Houghton, 1942. What happened around the cottonwood sapling—found by an Indian boy in 1610, protected as it grew by other Indians, reverenced as a Peace Medicine tree—is to a large extent the story of the Santa Fe trail. The fine full-page pictures in color show the country changing as the tree grew old. Many marginal drawings show Indian crafts, ox yokes, and wagons; and a large colored map marks the homes of Indian tribes. Ages 8–12.

James, Will. *Lone Cowboy, My Life Story;* il. by the author. Scribner, 1930. The autobiography of a real cowboy—horse-breaking and life on the range, his service in the army, and finally how he "started in on the art game"! Ages 12–15.

Parkman, Francis. *The Oregon Trail;* new ed.; il. by James Daugherty. Farrar, 1942. True account of the adventures of the author and his four companions on the western plains in 1846. Ages 12–15.

Rollins, Philip Ashton. *Jinglebob;* with il. in colors by N. C. Wyeth. Scribner, 1930. A story about a real cowboy who drove a herd of cattle from Texas to Montana in the 1880's. Ages 12–15.

Tousey, Sanford. *Cowboy Tommy;* il. by the author. Doubleday, 1932. A picture-story book about the true adventures of a little boy on a Texas ranch a generation ago. Easy to read and very popular with boys of today. *Cowboy Tommy's Round-Up* (Doubleday, 1934) is a sequel. Ages 6–8.

CHAPTER XXXI

South and Central America

Goetz, Delia. *Half a Hemisphere; the Story of Latin America;* il. with drawings by Charlotte Anna Chase, and with maps. Harcourt, 1943. A brief, well-written, authoritative history of Latin America. Ages 12–15.

Lansing, Marion. *Liberators and Heroes of South America;* il. by Paul Quinn. Page, 1940. Well-written, inspiring sketches of Bolivar, Miranda, San Martin, O'Higgins, and twelve other men who fought and planned for freedom in South America. Ages 11–15.

Malkus, Alida Sims. *The Citadel of a Hundred Stairways;* il. by Henry C. Pitz. Winston, 1941. Mrs. Malkus shows us an ancient city of Peru and certain exciting events which take place there through the eyes of two boys, one a Peruvian Indian and one the son of an American engineer mining for gold. The background is authentic, and the drawings by Henry Pitz have a fine adventurous quality. Ages 10–12.

Morris, Ann Axtell. *Digging in Yucatan;* il. by Jean Charlot. Doubleday, 1931. A lively, informal account of the author's experiences with the archaeological party sent out by the Carnegie Institution in 1924, when Chichen Itza was explored and the Maya Temple of Old Warriors re-erected. Ages 12–15.

Newcomb, Covelle. *Black Fire: A Story of Henri Christophe;* il. by Avery Johnson. Longmans, 1940. Story of the slave boy in the British West Indies who led the Haitian rebellion and became King Henry I of Haiti. Based on history. Ages 12–14.

Peck, Anne Merriman. *The Pageant of South American History.* Longmans, 1941. A history of South America from the days of the ancient civilizations to the present. Ages 12–14.

Shields, Karena. *Three in the Jungle;* il. by Harold Petersen. Harcourt, 1944. The adventures of three children during a summer in Chiapas in Central America. The author, who knows the country well, has filled her book with jungle atmosphere and jungle lore. Ages 9–12.

Shippen, Katherine. *New Found World;* il. by C. B. Falls. Viking, 1945. The geography and people of the Latin American countries, and their history from prehistoric times down to the present. The author, writing with imagination, interest, and real knowledge, has enriched her book with fascinating details and pertinent quotations from source material. Ages 10–15.

CHAPTER XXXII

All Quarters of the Globe

DISTANT horizons beckon, and with books at hand no one need be a stay-at-home.

Akeley, Mary L. Jobe. *Carl Akeley's Africa;* il.; foreword by Henry Fairfield Osborn. Dodd, 1930. Mrs. Akeley went across deserts of East Africa and through Uganda to the Congo with her husband on his last expedition. Ages 12–15.

Andrews, Roy Chapman. *Ends of the Earth;* il. Putnam, 1929. Accounts of expeditions to the Dutch East Indies, Korea, China, and other "ends of the earth" by an explorer and scientist who can write. Ages 12–15.

Beebe, William. *Exploring with Beebe; Selections for Younger Readers from the Writings of the Author;* il. with photographs by the author. Putnam, 1932. Five chapters from Galápagos, two from *The Arcturus Adventure,* and one each from *Beneath Tropic Seas, Jungle Days,* and *Pheasant Jungles.* Ages 12–14.

Beebe, William. *Jungle Peace.* Holt, 1918. This naturalist writes of his experiences in the South American jungle with enthusiasm, sympathy, and humor. Ages 12–14.

Busoni, Rafaello. *Stanley's Africa;* il. by the author. Viking, 1944. Not only Stanley's life and his dramatic meeting with Livingstone, but the mysterious continent itself, its history, and its peoples, is to be found in this authentic and absorbing book. Ages 12–15.

Byrd, Richard Evelyn. *Little America; Aerial Exploration in the Antarctic; the Flight to the South Pole;* with il. and maps. Putnam, 1930. Fascinating account of the largest expedition that ever wintered in the Antarctic. Ages 12–15.

Ellsworth, Lincoln. *Exploring Today*. Dodd, 1935. Various types of exploration from the North Pole to the South Seas discussed by a well-known explorer. Pictures by courtesy of the American Museum of Natural History. Ages 11–14.

Follett, Helen. *Ocean Outposts;* il. with maps by Armstrong Sperry and photographs. Scribner, 1942. In a style that is direct, lively, and touched with humor, the author describes the islands of the Pacific—Guam, Tahiti, Samoa, and the rest—giving their history, much about the life of the races that inhabit them, their industries and products, and their importance as military and supply bases, harbors, and airports in the recent war. In *Islands on Guard* (Scribner, 1943), Mrs. Follett discusses the islands of the Caribbean Sea. Both books are illustrated by beautiful photographs and have excellent maps. Ages 11–15.

Fox, Lorene K. *Antarctic Icebreakers;* il. with photographs; foreword by L. M. Gould. Doubleday, 1937. Beginning with the earliest known voyages made by sealers and whalers, the author continues with the expeditions of Scott, Amundsen, Shackleton, to Byrd, Wilkins, and Ellsworth. Simple, readable style, maps, and many excellent photographs. Ages 12–14.

Gatti, Ellen and Attilio. *Here Is Africa;* il. with photographs; maps by Raymond Lufkin. Scribner, 1943. Many beautiful photographs, and a text by two explorers which describes in readable fashion the different regions of the continent. Ages 10–14.

Hewes, Agnes. *Two Oceans to Canton; the Story of the Old China Trade*. Knopf, 1944. Vividly told story of America's China trade from the middle of the eighteenth century to the signing of the Wanghia Treaty in 1844. Ages 12–15.

Hogarth, Grace. *Australia, the Island Continent;* from material supplied by Joan Colebrook; il. by Howard W. Willard. Houghton, 1943. Clear, accurate presentation of the geography and the people of Australia, and its colorful history from Captain Cook's discovery of Botany Bay to the present. Ages 9–14.

Johnson, Martin. *Safari; a Saga of the African Blue*. Putnam, 1928. Lively descriptions of stalking elephants, lions, leopards, rhinoceroses, and other game in Africa, near Mt. Kenya. Splendid photographs of the animals at close range. Ages 12–15.

Kennedy, Jean. *Here Is India;* il. by photographs. Scribner, 1945. The author, who has lived in India, writes sympathetically and informally of the people, climate, religions, caste system, customs, and how India makes a living. Ages 14–15. Manorama Modak's *The Land and People of India,* il. by photographs (Lippincott, 1945), in the Portraits of the Nations series, writes from the point of view of an Indian citizen and interprets India's culture, ideals, and aspirations to become a democratic nation in the New World. Ages 10–14.

Nourse, Mary Augusta and Goetz, Delia. *China; Country of Contrasts;* il. with photographs. Harcourt, 1944. An interesting, intimate picture of China, written with young people's interests in mind. Ages 12–15.

Sondergaard, Arensa. *My First Geography of the Americas;* il. by Fritz Kredel. Little, 1942. Without overcrowding her pages with information, the author has built up for the seven- to nine-year-olds a background which will make all that they will hear later about the two continents more meaningful. Maps and many pictures. Ages 7–9.

Spencer, Cornelia. *Made in China; the Story of China's Expression;* with a foreword by Lin Yutang; il. by Kurt Wiese. Knopf, 1943. The author, who knows China well, as she covers a wide range of subjects, indicates the scope of the contribution made by China to civilization. Ages 12–15.

Stefansson, Evelyn. *Here Is Alaska;* with a foreword by Vilhjálmur Stefansson; with photographs by Frederick Machetanz and others. Scribner, 1943. Interesting description of the country and the Eskimos, based on research which has been done for Pan American Airways and the United States Army. Many unusual and beautiful photographs. Ages 10–15.

Stefansson, Evelyn. *Within the Circle; Portrait of the Arctic;* maps by Richard Edes Harrison; il. from photographs. Scribner, 1945. Stimulating account of how people live and work north of the Arctic. Ages 10–14.

Stefansson, Vilhjalmur. *Hunters of the Great North.* Harcourt, 1922. Mr. Stefansson tells how he became an Arctic explorer and describes the first winter and summer that he spent in the north. Ages 12–15.

Strong, Anna Louise. *Peoples of the USSR;* il. with photographs. Macmillan, 1944. Geography, natural resources, industries, history, political development, and racial groups of the sixteen republics that make up the Soviet Union. Ages 12–15.

Turley, Charles. *The Voyages of Captain Scott;* retold from *The Voyage of the Discovery,* and *Scott's Last Expedition;* with an introduction by Sir J. M. Barrie. Dodd, 1915. Contains a reproduction of Scott's last record in his diary and his farewell letters. This modern hero story draws a fine portrait of a courageous, lovable man. Ages 12–15.

Van Loon, Hendrik Willem. *Van Loon's Geography; the Story of the World We Live In;* written and il. by Hendrik Willem Van Loon. Garden City Pub. Co., 1940. What the author calls "a sort of human interest story applied to geography"; the people who live in the different parts of the earth, why they are there, where they came from, and what they are doing. Ages 12–14.

CHAPTER XXXIII

Ships and the Sea

Conrad, Joseph. *Typhoon and Other Stories.* Doubleday, 1903. The title story contains one of the greatest descriptions of a storm at sea ever written. Ages 14–15.

Dana, Richard Henry. *Two Years Before the Mast;* a personal narrative, with a supplement by the author and introduction and additional chapter by his son; il. by E. Boyd Smith. Houghton, 1911. (Riverside Bookshelf.) Written in 1840, this account of a voyage around the Horn and to California is the best picture there is of life on the old American sailing ships. Ages 12–14.

Edmonds, Mary D. *Out of the Net;* pictures by Dorothy Bayley. Oxford, 1940. Fine story of a fisher family in Newfoundland, with plenty of human interest, adventure, and excitement. Ages 11–14.

Hawes, Charles Boardman. *The Mutineers; a Tale of Old Days at Sea and of Adventures in the Far East as Benjamin Lathrop Set It Down Some Sixty Years Ago.* Little, 1930. The young hero's experiences as a green hand on a cargo vessel bound for China and the part he played during a time of mutiny and murder makes absorbing reading. Other good sea stories by this author are *Dark Frigate,* il. by A. O. Fischer (Little, 1924), and *The Great Quest,* il. by George Varian (Little, 1921). Ages 11–14.

Hurd, Edith Thacher. *The Wreck of the* Wild Wave; *Being the True Account of the Wreck of the Clipper Ship* Wild Wave *of Boston;* il. by F. T. Chapman. Oxford, 1942. Based on the log of an actual clipper ship which was wrecked on an uncharted reef in the South Seas when sailing from San Francisco in 1858. Seven of the crew landed on Pitcairn's Island, where they found that the inhabitants had been removed. Told in the first person by the ship's captain. Ages 12–15.

Kipling, Rudyard. *Captains Courageous.* Doubleday, 1897. Kipling's story of the spoiled son of an American millionaire who was washed overboard off the Newfoundland Banks. Picked up by a fishing smack and forced to work his way, he finally came out of the experience greatly improved. This book is perennially popular with boys and girls. Ages 11–13.

Masefield, John. *The Bird of Dawning; or, The Fortune of the Sea.* Macmillan, 1933. The author, a poet and sailor, has made this story of a sailing-ship race from the Pagoda Anchorage to the Thames an extraordinarily vivid picture of the sea, ships, and the men who sail them. Ages 12–15.

Melville, Herman. *Moby Dick; or, The White Whale;* il. by Mead Schaeffer. Dodd, 1922. This tale of the ill-fated vessel that sought Moby Dick, the white whale, through the Seven Seas, is a classic description of whaling in the days of the old "three-masters." Ages 12–15.

Nordhoff, Charles B. and Hall, James N. *Mutiny on the Bounty.* Little, 1932. Based on Admiralty records, this book written in admirable prose with a fine eighteenth-century flavor, tells the strange history of H.M.S. *Bounty,* which sailed from England in 1787 bound for Tahiti. The sequel, *Men Against the Sea* (Little, 1934), tells the story of Captain Bligh and the eighteen loyal men who sailed 3600 miles in an open boat. Ages 12–15.

Pease, Howard. *The Tattooed Man; a Tale of Strange Adventures Befalling Tod Moran, Mess Boy of the Tramp Steamer* Araby *upon His First Voyage from San Francisco to Genoa, via the Panama Canal;* il. by Mahlon Blaine. Sun Dial, 1937. (Young Moderns Bookshelf.) *The Jinx Ship* (Sun Dial, 1927) and several other stories by this author continue the adventures of Tod Moran. Ages 10–14.

Smith, Cicely Fox. *The Ship Aground; a Tale of Adventure;* il. by C. Walter Hodges. Oxford, 1941. What happened to fourteen-year-old Barty Dale when he was shanghaied as a ship's boy on a vessel bound out of England for the west coast of America in the early years of the nineteenth century. A sea story with real flavor and quality. Ages 11–14.

Sperry, Armstrong. *All Sail Set: a Romance of the* Flying Cloud; written and il. by Armstrong Sperry; introd. by William Mc-Fee. Winston, 1935. Young Enoch Thacher, who worked for Donald McKay, famous designer and builder of the *Flying Cloud,* and later shipped aboard her as apprentice seaman, tells the story of the clipper's maiden voyage around the Horn. Ages 11–14.

Stevenson, Robert Louis. *Treasure Island;* il. by N. C. Wyeth. Scribner, 1924. (Scribner Illustrated Classics.) Style, character drawing, atmosphere, excitement, and mystery all go to make this one of the best and most absorbing tales of pirates and buried treasure ever written. Ages 10–14.

Verne, Jules. *Twenty Thousand Leagues under the Sea;* il. by W. J. Aylward. Scribner. (Scribner Illustrated Classics.) First published in 1870. Captain Nemo and his submarine boat existed in the imagination of an ingenious Frenchman long before the submarine was invented. *The Mysterious Island* (Scribner, 1918) is a sequel. Ages 10–14.

Villiers, Alan J. *Whalers of the Midnight Sun; a Story of Modern Whaling in the Antarctic;* il. by Charles Pont. Scribner, 1934. A stirring adventure story based on the author's own experience with whales and whalers in the South Seas. Ages 12–14.

CHAPTER XXXIV

Out-of-Doors

IN THE midst of the busy life of a city, boys and girls, as well as their elders, forget or perhaps never become aware of larger happenings that take place every day; country dwellers often accept them as a matter of course. Books, then, about the out-of-doors perform a real service when they remind us of the procession of the seasons, of the stars that shine even over city streets, and the changes of the moon, of the clouds and sunsets, the new green leaves in spring, or the beauty of bare branches and snow-covered fields in winter.

Fenton, Carroll Lane. *Along Nature's Highway;* with il. by the author. Day, 1943. A provocative little book on the beasts, birds, insects, and plants which may be seen when the traveler takes, not the main traveled routes where trucks and busses run, but the quiet roads that go past farms and rocky pastures, follow streams, or wind among the hills. Age 10 on.

Hylander, C. J. *Out of Doors in Spring.* Macmillan, 1942. *Out of Doors in Summer.* Macmillan, 1942. *Out of Doors in Autumn.* Macmillan, 1942. *Out of Doors in Winter.* Macmillan, 1943. Each volume illustrated by the author, who is thoroughly familiar with the outdoor world and writes about it with directness, clarity, and a quiet enthusiasm that is contagious. His book will be very useful to those who wish to know more about the life they see around them if they are fortunate enough to live in the country. Even those who must be content with what they can observe in parks, aquariums, and city gardens will find these volumes stimulating. *The Year Round; a Book of the Out of Doors Arranged According to Season,* by the same author (Putnam, 1932), is a year-round guide to the most common minerals, plants, and animals to be found in the country or at the seashore. Age 10 on.

Pocket Nature Library. 4 v. Doubleday. v.1, *Wild Flowers East of the Rockies,* by Chester A. Reed. 1916. v.2. *Land Birds East of the Rockies,* by Chester A. Reed. 1906. v.3, *Butterfly Guide,* by W. J. Holland. 1915. v.4, *Tree Guide,* by Julia Ellen Rogers. 1905. Convenient little manuals for identification which children can readily use. Age 9 on.

CHAPTER XXXV

The Heavens

Baker, Robert H. *When the Stars Come Out.* Viking, 1934. To read Dr. Baker's book is like having a wise, enthusiastic friend sit down beside you and answer your questions about the heavens. *Introducing the Constellations* (Viking, 1937), by the same author, tells how to identify the constellations, and gives stories and legends connected with them. Ages 11–14.

Frost, Edwin Brant. *Let's Look at the Stars;* il. Houghton, 1935. The author, who was for many years director of the Yerkes Observatory, describes simply sun, moon, eclipses, planets, comets, meteors, and constellations, and the methods by which they are studied. Ages 10–13.

Meyer, Jerome S. *Picture Book of Astronomy;* il. by Richard Floethe. Lothrop, 1945. Some of the basic astronomical facts presented to children in terms of their own experience, with accuracy, imagination, and humor. The spirited drawings are an integral part of a text which "has succeeded in the difficult task of relating astronomy to a child's own world." Ages 8–10.

Reed, William Maxwell. *The Stars for Sam;* ed. by C. E. St. John; il. by Karl Moseley. Harcourt, 1931. Emphasizes the new discoveries which are constantly enlarging man's knowledge of astronomy. Well illustrated by many reproductions of photographs. Ages 10–14.

CHAPTER XXXVI

The Earth

Bretz, Rudolph. *How the Earth Is Changing.* Follett, 1936. (The Story of the World.) An easy geology, written in an interesting way. Ages 9–11.

Bruère, Martha Bensley. *Your Forests;* with a foreword by Gifford Pinchot; il. with photographs. Lippincott, 1945. What and where American forests are; how the U.S. Forest Service cares for and develops them; how these forests are conserved, increased, harvested, and used for our benefit in a multitude of ways: all of this is included in Mrs. Bruère's well-written, interesting book. Age 12 on.

Coleman, Satis N. *Volcanoes New and Old;* il. by photographs. Day, 1945. One of the most exciting and fascinating of natural phenomena, described with charm and enthusiasm and illustrated with unusual and beautiful photographs. Age 10 on.

Fenton, Carroll Lane and Mildred Adams. *The Land We Live On.* Doubleday, 1944. Each page of text, describing the land and how it changes, is accompanied by a full-page photograph showing hills and valleys, plains, prairies, mesas, rivers, islands, and deserts. Ages 9–12.

Fenton, Carroll Lane and Mildred Adams, *Mountains;* il. with photographs and drawings by the authors. Doubleday, 1942. A splendidly informative book about the mountains in North America, with special emphasis on the western ranges. The authors present every phase in the history of mountain building, explaining "blister mountains," lava flows and volcanoes, sedimentary rocks, glaciers, the ice age, and process of weathering. There are chapters on plant and animal life. Illustrated by clear diagrams and drawings and beautiful photographs, some in color. Ages 12–15. In his *Along the Hill* (Day, 1935), for somewhat younger readers, Carroll Lane Fenton gives a clear account of the formation of different types of rock which form the earth's surface as we know it today. Ages 9–12.

Reed, William Maxwell. *The Earth for Sam; the Story of Mountains, Rivers, Dinosaurs, and Men;* il. by Karl Moseley. Harcourt, 1932. A child's history of the earth through successive geologic periods, written by a former professor of astronomy for his nine-year-old nephew. Ages 9–13.

Zim, Herbert S. and Cooper, Elizabeth K. *Minerals: Their Identification, Uses and How to Collect Them.* Harcourt, 1943. What the amateur mineralogist needs to know is in this book. Ages 9–15.

CHAPTER XXXVII

The Sea

Brindze, Ruth. *The Gulf Stream;* il. by Helène Carter. Vanguard, 1945. Here the Gulf Stream is presented not merely as an ocean current or an explanation of climate but as a part of history, an "international highway for fish" and a "weather factory." Illustrated by beautiful drawings which show a feeling for the dramatic in nature. Ages 8–12.

Butler, Mrs. Eva L. *Along the Shore;* il. by the author. Day, 1930. Simple description of the small creatures, flowers, and birds found along the shore and in tide pools. Clear drawings. Ages 9–13.

Reed, William Maxwell and Bronson, Wilfrid S. *The Sea for Sam;* ed. by F. C. Brown and C. M. Breder, Jr.; il. by W. S. Bronson. Harcourt, 1935. The origin of the oceans, the rise and fall of continents, tides and undersea life, described in interesting fashion, with excellent illustrations. Ages 10–13.

CHAPTER XXXVIII

The Weather

Gaer, Joseph. *Everybody's Weather*. Lippincott, 1944. Rhymes, old proverbs, and scientific information about the weather, accompanied by beautiful photographs. Ages 9–15.

Heile, Maryanna. *World's Moods*. Rockwell, 1930. (The Story of the World.) A simply written book on the weather. Ages 9–11.

Pickwell, Gayle Benjamin. *Weather*. McGraw, 1938. The phenomena of weather, man's efforts to foretell it, and his struggle to control wind, floods, and erosion. Forty-five notable pictures of clouds, storms, ice, and erosion. Ages 12–15.

CHAPTER XXXIX

Man's Scientific Discoveries about the World Around Us

De Kruif, Paul. *Microbe Hunters*. Harcourt, 1926. Biographical sketches of Leeuwenhoek, Pasteur, Metchnikoff, and others, whose epoch-making discoveries in bacteriology have made them famous. Ages 12–15.

Headstrom, Richard. *Adventures with a Microscope*. Stokes, 1941. Fifty-nine simple experiments show the possibilities of working with a microscope. The reader is told how to find material, how to study it, what he will see, and what it means. Ages 11–15.

Huey, Edward Greene. *What Makes the Wheels Go Round; a First Time Physics;* il. by Edward Loemker. Reynal, 1940. Beginning with the electron and atom the author describes the phenomena of light, heat, electricity, magnetism, and gravity; also batteries, motors, engines, generators, and other applications of primary forces. Ages 10–13.

Nechaev, I. *Chemical Elements;* trans. from the Russian by Beatrice Kinkead. Coward-McCann, 1942. How the elements were discovered and something about the men who discovered them. Ages 12–15.

Pollak, Janet. *This Physical World*. Rockwell, 1930. (The Story of the World.) Tells simply of gravity, heat, motion, sound, electricity. Ages 10–12.

Ratcliff, John D. *Yellow Magic; the Story of Penicillin*. Random House, 1945. The biography of this wonderful new drug, written in easy, nontechnical language. Ages 12–15.

111

Yates, Raymond F. *Atom Smashers; a Story of Discovery;* il. with thirty-three drawings and photographs. Didier, 1945. The author tells in nontechnical language the story of the atom from early days to the present and explains the atom bomb. Ages 12–15.

Zim, Herbert Spencer. *Rockets and Jets;* il. with drawings by James MacDonald and with photographs. Harcourt, 1945. The history, design, and use of rockets and jets, told in readable, simple fashion. Ages 12–15.

CHAPTER XL

People You Might Meet

THERE is keen pleasure in meeting in books people much like ourselves, people the author has made so real that we feel we could step into the next street or go to the next town and find them there.

Alcott, Louisa May. *Little Women;* il. in color by J. W. Smith. Little, 1929. (Beacon Hill Bookshelf.) For nearly a hundred years, the adventures of the March family in *Little Women* have warmed the hearts of readers all over the world. *Little Men* (Little, 1924), which follows *Little Women, Eight Cousins* (Little, 1927), *Old-Fashioned Girl* (Little, 1926), and *Under the Lilacs* (Little, 1928), are other well-loved stories by this author. Ages 9–13.

Angelo, Valenti. *Hill of Little Miracles;* written and il. by Valenti Angelo. Viking, 1942. A story of an Italian family in San Francisco, true to life, and touched with genuine humor and kindliness. The book gives a sense of living, of everyday happiness, and of the enjoyment of simple things. Throughout, we feel the personality of Ricci, the boy who already had the seeing eye and understanding spirit of the artist he wanted to be. The drawings have the clear, sensitive beauty of the story. Ages 9–13.

Angelo, Valenti. *The Rooster Club;* il. by the author. Viking, 1944. A group of Boy Scouts hike, camp, sail, and harvest beans with gusto, vigor, and good humor, in a fine spirit of comradeship. Ages 9–12.

Bacon, Frances A. *Turkey Tale;* il. by Grace Paull. Oxford, 1935. The true story of a white turkey in Baltimore and how he escaped playing the central role at Thanksgiving. There is genuine humor in both text and pictures. Ages 7–9.

Barne, Kitty. *We'll Meet in England;* il. by Steven Spurrier. Dodd, 1943. Fifteen-year-old Hertha Larson and her brother Rudy escape from Norway under the eyes of a Nazi agent, sailing across the sea in a cockleshell of a boat in order to get to England and help in the fight to free Norway. A stirring story with excellent characterization. The author's *Three and a Pigeon,* il. by Stuart Tresilian (Dodd, 1944), tells in the same lively, natural way a story of English children in wartime and contains a fine portrait of a London cockney child. *In the Same Boat,* il. by Ruth Gervis (Dodd, 1945), tells of the friendship of a little Polish girl and an English girl in wartime England. Ages 9–13.

Bechdolt, Jack and Merwin, Decie. *Dulcie and Half a Yard of Linsey-Woolsey.* Dutton, 1943. Little children like to read of catastrophes, and they will be amused by Dulcie's mild difficulties. They will also be entertained by the way the narrative now and again breaks into rhyme. The drawings of early nineteenth-century boys and girls have grace and gaiety and a delicate childlike charm. Other books about Dulcie by the same authors are *Dulcie and the Donkey* (Dutton, 1944) and *Dulcie Sews a Sampler* (Dutton, 1945). Ages 6–9.

Bianco, Mrs. Margery W. *Bright Morning;* drawings by Margaret Platt. Viking, 1942. A story of two little girls, aged eight and five, who lived in London when Queen Victoria, a little old lady dressed in black, rode through the streets in her carriage. Writing with perception and quiet humor, the author has captured the feeling of the period and the quality of early childhood when sensation is fresh and keen and every experience intensely interesting. Ages 9–12.

Bianco, Mrs. Margery W. *Other People's Houses.* Viking, 1939. The story of Dale Forrest, who faces the world on her own and makes good. A normal, average, eighteen-year-old girl, with no special training or unusual gifts, she has pluck and a sense of humor, interest in people, a determination to try anything, domestic jobs included, rather than give in. Her job-hunting experiences in New York make good reading. Ages 10–13.

Bianco, Mrs. Margery W. *Winterbound.* Viking, 1936. A well-written, natural story of four young people from the city, who find fun and satisfaction in adjusting themselves to a winter in the Connecticut hills and the problems of homemaking. Ages 10–13.

Cather, Willa Sibert. *My Antonia;* with il. by W. T. Benda. Houghton, 1918. Against the background of pioneer Nebraska, Antonia, a shy Bohemian girl, acquires the strength to cope with more than physical hardships. Ages 12–15.

Caudill, Rebecca. *Barrie & Daughter;* il. by Berkeley Williams, Jr. Viking, 1943. How Fern Barrie helped her father open a store for honest trading in the Kentucky Mountain country a generation ago. This fresh, unusual story has a fine integrity and emphasizes true values. Ages 12–15.

Chalmers, Audrey. *Lolly;* il. by the author. Oxford, 1938. Lolly is a genuine and endearing small boy, and the people of the little Canadian town in which he lived are very real. The drawings have the same humor and imagination and fine characterization as the text. Ages 8–11.

Chute, B. J. *Shattuck Cadet;* pictures by Raymond Lufkin. Macmillan, 1940. A school story with genuine characterization and humor. The setting is a well-known military academy in Minnesota. Ages 10–13.

Chute, B. J. *Shift to the Right; a Collection of Sport Stories;* decorations by John C. Wonsetler. Macmillan, 1944. Nine stories in which the characters are made as real and vivid as the sports. Ages 10–13.

Clymer, Eleanor. *A Yard for John;* with pictures by Mildred Boyle. McBride, 1943. John, who lived in a city apartment, longed for mud to dig in, a swing, and grass, and when his father and mother moved into a little white house out of town, he had all those things. A story of real life touched with the magic with which unspoiled childhood invests the affairs of daily living. Ages 6–8.

Coatsworth, Elizabeth. *Alice-All-by-Herself;* pictures by Marguerite de Angeli. Macmillan, 1937. An appealing story of a thoughtful, imaginative little girl, with a small town in Maine as background. Ages 9–11.

Coatsworth, Elizabeth. *Away Goes Sally;* il. by Helen Sewell. Macmillan, 1934. The small heroine has the novel and exhilarating experience of traveling with her three aunts all the way from Hingham, Massachusetts, to the Penobscot River, in a little house built by her uncle Joshua and drawn on a sledge by six yoke of oxen. The story is told with an imaginative feeling for the New England country in winter and a humorous and kindly understanding of the characters described. *Five Bushel Farm* (Macmillan, 1939), *The Fair American* (Macmillan, 1940), and *The White Horse* (Macmillan, 1942) tell more of Sally's adventures. Ages 9–11.

Coatsworth, Elizabeth. *The Littlest House;* il. by Marguerite Davis. Macmillan, 1940. A story of two little girls and a very small boy. They discover a tiny gray house in a little street in a town by the sea, and are allowed to furnish it, call it their own, and use it for one long happy summer. *Twelve Months Make a Year,* il. by Marguerite Davis (Macmillan, 1943), continues the adventures of the same three children. In both stories the children are real. They have a sturdy honesty that is very engaging, and the gracious relationship between children and grownups is one of the charms of the book. Ages 8–10.

Coatsworth, Elizabeth. *Trudy and the Tree House;* il. by Marguerite Davis. Macmillan, 1944. Housekeeping, in the enchanting house built by an understanding father in an oak tree, was a delight to mischievous Trudy (though it did not always keep her out of trouble). Ages 9–12.

Comfort, Mildred Houghton. *Winter on the Johnny Smoker;* il. by Henry C. Pitz. Morrow, 1943. An authentic story of steamboating days in the late nineteenth century, told with freshness and charm. Ages 10–13.

Coolidge, Susan. *What Katy Did.* Little, 1924. (Beacon Hill Bookshelf.) Several generations of girls have enjoyed these still popular stories of high-spirited, impulsive Katie and her brothers and sisters. Other books by this author are: *What Katy Did at School* (Little, 1927), *What Katy Did Next* (Little, 1930), *Clover* (Little, 1913), *In the High Valley* (Little, 1909). Ages 9–12.

Cormack, Maribelle and Alexander, W. P. *Wind of the Vikings; a Tale of the Orkney Isles;* il. by Robert Lawson. Appleton-Century, 1937. A young girl comes from New York to stay with her father's people in the Orkney Isles, where she makes friends and finds romance. Good characterization and authentic atmosphere. Ages 11–14.

Credle, Ellis. *Down Down the Mountain.* Nelson, 1934. Large drawings and a pleasant little story of two children and a pair of new shoes picture life in the Blue Ridge Mountains. Ages 8–9.

Cregan, Máirín. *Rathina;* il. by Flora Nash DeMuth. Macmillan, 1942. Delightful story of Irish home life. The Donovans were outdoor people, and horses and dogs play an important part in the lives of the four children. A book with atmosphere and excellent characterization. Ages 10–13.

Dalgliesh, Alice. *The Silver Pencil;* decorations by Katherine Milhous. Scribner, 1944. Beginning in Trinidad when the heroine is ten, the scene changes to England. Later the girl comes to America to be trained as a teacher and a writer. At the end of the story she has written her second book, built a house with the royalties from her first one, and become an American citizen. The author has drawn on her own experiences. Ages 10–14.

De Angeli, Marguerite. *Up the Hill.* Doubleday, 1942. The story of ten-year-old Polish Aniela, her family, and friends, who live in a small mining town in Pennsylvania. There are many lovely pictures, and the background of the story is rich in suggestions of national customs, legends, and music. *Henner's Lydia* (Doubleday, 1936) and *Yonie Wondernose* (Doubleday, 1944), written and illustrated by the same author, are picture-story books of the Pennsylvania Dutch country. *Yonie Wondernose* is for children 6–8. Ages 8–10.

Emerson, Caroline D. *Father's Big Improvements;* il. by Margaret Ayer. Stokes, 1936. This paints a pleasant picture of family life in the 1890's, and in describing how one modern improvement after another was installed by the energetic father of the family, it serves as a brief chronicle of the progress of the machine age. The spontaneous humor and the human nature in the story make it excellent for reading aloud. Ages 8–10.

Enright, Elizabeth. *The Saturdays;* il. by the author. Farrar, 1941. Four children make their own plan for spending their allowances on successive Saturdays. Told with humor and genuine characterization. Followed by the equally successful *Four Story Mistake* (Farrar, 1942), and *Then There Were Five* (Farrar, 1944). *Thimble Summer* (Farrar, 1938), by the same author, is a refreshingly spontaneous story of a very real little girl on a Wisconsin farm of today. Ages 9–12.

Estes, Eleanor. *The Moffats;* il. by Louis Slobodkin. Harcourt, 1941. There was very little money to spend, but life was always interesting for the four young Moffats, aged from five and a half to fifteen. Followed by *The Middle Moffat.* Harcourt, 1942. Ages 9–11.

Field, Rachel Lyman. *Hepatica Hawks;* il. by Allen Lewis. Macmillan, 1932. A fine study of a girl in the 1890's. Hepatica at fifteen was six feet four and one-half inches tall and formed part of a traveling circus. Material out of the beaten track, which the author has handled with delicacy and sincerity. Ages 12–15.

Gates, Doris. *Blue Willow;* il. by Paul Lantz. Viking, 1940. Well thought out story of ten-year-old Janey Larkin, only child of a migrating family of the San Joaquin Valley. Ages 9–12.

Gates, Doris. *Sarah's Idea;* il. by Marjorie Torrey. Viking, 1938. About a delightful tomboy who wanted nothing so much as a burro—and got it. Ages 8–11.

Gates, Doris. *Sensible Kate;* il. by Marjorie Torrey. Viking, 1943. A spirited, human story of a natural, engaging little girl who, being a sensible child, did not very much mind being a county charge, and won for herself, in the end, a home where she was loved and needed. Ages 9–12.

Gordon, Patricia. *The Boy Jones;* with drawings by Adrienne Adams. Viking, 1944. The story of the boy who, uninvited and unknown, lived in Buckingham Palace, is a refreshingly original mixture of Victorian London and sedate, though quite spontaneous nonsense. A fantasy based on fact. Ages 10–14.

Grahame, Kenneth. *Golden Age;* il. by E. H. Shepard. Dodd, 1929. First published in 1895, this remains one of the classic books about children. Its delightful humor and understanding of human nature are enjoyed by many boys and girls and by adults. *Dream Days,* il. by E. H. Shepard (Dodd, 1931), is a second book about the same characters. Ages 12–15.

Gray, Elizabeth Janet. *The Fair Adventure;* il. by Alice K. Reischer. Viking, 1940. A story of today with a delightfully real and lovable heroine. Page MacNeil, the youngest of the five young MacNeils, wants to go to a distant college. How she plans and struggles, during the summer after high-school graduation, to find a way of carrying out her ambition, makes a thoroughly readable story, told with humor and fine characterization. *Jane Hope* (Viking, 1938), by the same author, is a convincing story of a twelve-year-old girl in North Carolina just before the Civil War, full of humor and human nature. Ages 12–14.

Gray, Elizabeth Janet. *Sandy.* Viking, 1945. Seventeen-year-old Sandy, breezy, impetuous, full of the restlessness and uncertainties that beset girls of her years, has a fine honesty and a sense of humor that carry her through the difficulties which assail her and which are sometimes of her own making. Ages 12–14.

Haines, Donal H. *The Fortress, a Story of Hilton Academy.* Farrar, 1945. A school story which, along with a lively account of the building up of a winning baseball team, has substance, integrity, and a refreshing note of idealism. Ages 11–14.

Haines, Donal H. *Sporting Chance.* Farrar, 1935. A well-written story which shows how George Colby, son of a millionaire, after going through experiences which entirely transformed his lot in life, was changed from a selfish, unpopular boy to a self-reliant, likable young man. Ages 10–14.

Holberg, Ruth Langland. *Tibby's Venture;* il. by Phyllis N. Coté. Doubleday, 1943. The story of a little girl who lived on Cape Anne more than fifty years ago, told with humor and understanding. One senses in the tale the joy and excitement felt in Cape Cod families when the seafaring head of the household returned after a long voyage. Ages 9–12.

Honness, Elizabeth. *The Great Gold Piece Mystery;* pictures by Eloise Wilkins. Oxford, 1944. Outdoor atmosphere, fine family relationships, and a mystery that is solved in a credible manner by three unspoiled, natural children. Ages 9–12.

Hunt, Mabel Leigh. *Lucinda, a Little Girl of 1860;* il. by Cameron Wright. Stokes, 1934. Imaginatively told story of a little Quaker girl in Indiana before the Civil War. Ages 9–12.

Jordan, Mildred. *Shoo-Fly Pie;* il. by Henry C. Pitz. Knopf, 1944. A story of Dutch Pennsylvania farm life with a lively eight-year-old heroine who never meant to be naughty but whose ingenuity in thinking up things to do led her into escapades and misadventures which are relished by child readers. Ages 8–11.

Judson, Clara Ingram. *They Came from Sweden;* il. by Edward C. Caswell. Houghton, 1942. A very human story of one of the sturdy Swedish families who settled the Northwest. Old and young shared in the heroic labor, the self-denial, and the steadfast purpose which were needed in making a home in a new country. Fourteen-year-old Gustaf helped to bridge the gap between the New World and the Old by studying English from a weekly newspaper. Also, *They Came from Scotland,* il. by Mary A. Reardon (Houghton, 1944); *They Came from Dalmatia, Petar's Treasure,* il. by Ursula Koering (Houghton, 1945); and *They Came from France* (Houghton, 1943). Ages 9–12.

Kästner, Erich. *Emil and the Detectives, a Story for Children;* trans. from the German by May Massee; il. by Walter Trier. Doubleday, 1930. A group of boys organize themselves into an amateur detective force to get back the money stolen from one of them on the train by a clever thief. There is mystery and suspense and a successful conclusion. The translation is natural and lively and the pictures amusing. Ages 8–12.

Kipling, Rudyard. *Stalky & Co.* Doubleday, 1899. Three English schoolboys come very much alive in Kipling's story, to remain so; for whether it is a twenty-first reading or a first, boys and girls and adults settle down with fresh enjoyment to follow the adventures and escapades of these irrepressibles. Ages 12–15.

Kristoffersen, Eva. *A Bee in Her Bonnet;* il. by Helen Sewell. Crowell, 1944. Rural Nebraska is the background for this genuinely American story of a little girl who is transplanted from the city to a farm, where she conquers her fears, learns to keep bees, and to do many other useful things successfully. Ages 9–12.

Kyle, Elisabeth. *Disappearing Island;* il. by Marjorie Quennell. Houghton, 1944. A fine outdoor story of holidays in the north of Scotland. A mystery is credibly solved, the life of the little village is described, and the brother and sister and the other characters of the story are well drawn and interesting. Ages 9–12.

Lenski, Lois. *Bayou Suzette;* il. by the author. Lippincott, 1943. A tale set in the Louisiana Bayou country about a little white girl and a little Indian girl whom she takes home to become a member of the family. *Strawberry Girl,* by the same author (Lippincott, 1945), is another authentic regional story which tells of a little Florida Cracker girl. Ages 8–11.

Lenski, Lois. *Blueberry Corners; Story and Pictures.* Stokes, 1940. Life in a country parsonage in Connecticut a hundred years ago, where there were eight children. It was hard to make ends meet, luxuries were non-existent, and new clothes something to be dreamed of and rarely attained. Nevertheless, natural cheerfulness, a sense of humor, and warm family affection gave zest and gaiety to a workaday world. Nine-year-old Becky, with whom the story is chiefly concerned, is a very real little girl. Ages 9–12.

Locklin, Anne Littlefield. *Tidewater Tales;* il. by Rafaello Busoni. Viking, 1942. Stories of a New Hampshire boyhood, so genuine, so full of human nature and humor, that children of today read them with pleasure and recognize the likeness between these mischievous, adventurous boys of an earlier day and themselves. Ages 8–12.

Lucas, E. V. *The Slowcoach.* Macmillan, 1910. The adventures of seven interesting children on their travels through the Shakespeare country in a caravan, reads as well today as when it was first written. A good book to read aloud. Ages 10–12.

McCloskey, Robert. *Homer Price;* il. by the author. Viking, 1943. Half-a-dozen episodes in the life of a small-town boy who mended radios, caught burglars with the aid of his pet skunk Aroma, made an incredible number of doughnuts in his uncle's automatic doughnut-maker, and engaged in other adventures that delight boys and girls. There is wisdom as well as humor in the book, and the irresistible drawings are an integral part of the text. Ages 9–14.

Macdonald, Zillah. *Two on a Tow;* il. by Harvey Kidder. Houghton, 1942. A lively story of identical twins on the barge *Araminta,* where only one of them was supposed to be; orphans and unwilling to be separated, one of them stowed away. Unhackneyed, well-worked-out plot, full of surprises for the reader, and as background, a good picture of life in the old days of the New York State Barge Canal. Ages 10–13.

McNeely, Mrs. Marion Hurd. *The Jumping-Off Place;* il. by William Siegel. Longmans, 1929. The story of four orphans, aged eight to eighteen, who go to Dakota after their uncle's death to take up his claim. Warm-hearted, loyal family relationships, a genuine feeling for the land, and the ability to surmount difficulties, characterize this thoroughly American tale. Ages 11–14.

McSwigan, Marie. *Snow Treasure;* il. by Mary Reardon. Dutton, 1942. How boys and girls in Norway carried millions of dollars' worth of gold bullion on their sleds, down the hills and through the German camp, so that it could be shipped to the United States for safekeeping. Based on a true incident. Ages 8–13.

Mason, Miriam E. *Little Jonathan;* il. by George and Doris Hauman. Macmillan, 1944. The youngest of a family who lived in Indiana more than one hundred years ago is made very real, and while children are enjoying his adventures, they are absorbing many details of life in pioneer days. Ages 6–8.

Mason, Miriam E. *Smiling Hill Farm;* il. by Kate Seredy. Ginn, 1937. A story which shows, for the youngest readers, the development of American life on a farm from pioneer days to the present. Ages 8–10.

Meader, Stephen W. *Blueberry Mountain;* il. by Edward Shenton. Harcourt, 1941. Two farm boys in the Pocono Mountains undertake to have their own blueberry farm. In the process, they make both friends and enemies, but succeed in outwitting the schemes of the latter. A good story that incidentally tells much about blueberry culture. Ages 11–14.

Meader, Stephen W. *Red Horse Hill;* il. by Lee Townsend. Harcourt, 1930. A good story of an enterprising boy, against a background of New Hampshire life a generation ago, with much about horses and amateur horse racing. Ages 11–14.

Means, Florence Crannell. *Candle in the Mist;* il. by Marguerite de Angeli. Houghton, 1931. Pioneer life and its hardships, a mystery, and a courageous girl who enjoys life in spite of its difficulties and teaches school successfully at fifteen. Ages 10–13.

Milhous, Katherine. *Herodia, the Lovely Puppet;* il. by the author in color and in black and white. Scribner, 1942. The story of a real little girl who, in the 1870's, played the part of a marionette in a traveling puppet show. Based on an actual happening. The illustrations are gay and appealing. Ages 10–12.

North, Sterling. *Midnight and Jeremiah;* il. by Kurt Wiese. Winston, 1943. The story of an Indiana farm boy, told with sincerity and kindly humor. Ages 9–11.

Parton, Ethel. *Vinny Applegay, Her First Year in New York, a Story of the 1870's.* Viking, 1937. The story of a delightfully lifelike little girl, and a good picture of New York in the 1870's. Miss Parton's other five books, *Runaway Prentice* (Viking, 1939), *The Lost Locket* (Viking, 1940), *Penelope Ellen* (Viking, 1936), *The House Between* (Viking, 1943), and *The Year Without a Summer* (Viking, 1945), make a fine chronicle of life in New England in the first half of the nineteenth century. Ages 9–12.

Pease, Howard. *Thunderbolt House;* il. by Armstrong Sperry. Doubleday, 1944. A mystery story that makes San Francisco, in the year of the great fire, come alive. Good plot and unusual characters. Ages 9–12.

Ransome, Arthur. *Swallows and Amazons;* il. by Helène Carter. Lippincott, 1931. There are no better stories being written for young people today than Arthur Ransome's, with their irresistibly real and engaging boys and girls and their fine background of out-of-doors, camping, ships, and sailing. Other stories dealing with the same six boys and girls are *Swallowdale* (Lippincott, 1932), *Peter Duck* (Lippincott, 1933), *Winter Holiday* (Lippincott, 1934), *Missee Lee* (Macmillan, 1942), *The Picts and Martyrs; or, Not Welcome at All* (Macmillan, 1943). Ages 10–13.

Richards, Mrs. Laura E. *Queen Hildegarde.* Page, 1889. Though written many years ago, Mrs. Richards' story of the development of a girl's character and the new interests that came into her life after a summer spent in the country, rings true and is still enjoyed by girls of today. Other books about the same characters are *Hildegarde's Holiday* (Page, 1891); *Hildegarde's Home* (Page, 1892); and *Hildegarde's Harvest* (Page, 1897). Ages 10–12.

Robinson, Mabel Louise. *Bright Island;* with decorations by Lynd Ward. Random House, 1937. Thankful Curtis, daughter of a sea captain, left her home on an island off the coast of Maine to go to school on the mainland. It is, however, the island life that she chooses in the end. Good outdoor atmosphere. Ages 11–14.

Rounds, Glen. *Lumber Camp, Being the Life and Good Times of the New Whistle Punk at Camp Fifteen up Horse Crick Way;* many drawings made on the scene by the author. Holiday House, 1937. This, with the author's *Pay Dirt*, il. by the author (Holiday House, 1938), furnish lively and authentic accounts of distinctive parts of our country and characteristic occupations. The drawings have a fine humor. Ages 10–13.

Savery, Constance. *Enemy Brothers;* decorations by Henry Pitz. Longmans, 1943. A thoroughly interesting story, valuable for its picture of wartime England and its fine study of the English boy who had been brought up a Nazi and his brother, whose patience and understanding slowly brought about a change of heart and won the younger boy to the English way of life. Ages 12–15.

Sawyer, Ruth. *Roller Skates;* il. by Valenti Angelo. Viking, 1936. A book with reality, sparkle, and humor, which gives a picture of a delightful child in the New York of the 'Nineties. Adults, as well as children, enjoy Lucinda and her friends. The illustrations have caught the spirit of the text and suggest the city Lucinda knew. The author's *The Year of Jubilo*, drawings by Edward Shenton (Viking, 1940), tells of another year in Lucinda's life, when she was fifteen and the family went to live in a small town in Maine. Ages 10–13.

Sayers, Frances Clarke. *Tag-Along Tooloo;* il. by Helen Sewell. Viking, 1941. The story of a very real little girl who, wherever her older sister and her older sister's friends went, wanted to go along, too. A book with serenity, friendliness, and kindly atmosphere. Ages 6–10.

Seyfert, Ella Maie. *Little Amish School-House;* il. by Ninon MacKnight. Crowell, 1939. This little story of David and Martha

Wenger, their parents, and their grandfather, is told simply and naturally by someone who has lived among the Amish folk and writes of them with understanding and affection. A sympathetic presentation of an interesting and little-known group of people. Followed by *Amish Moving Day* (Crowell, 1942). Ages 8–11.

Sidney, Margaret. *Five Little Peppers and How They Grew;* il. by George Giguère. Houghton, 1937. (Riverside Bookshelf.) First published in 1881 but still read and loved, for though it describes a world without automobiles, radio, or airplanes, children recognize the reality and human quality of the characters. Ages 9–11.

Snedeker, Mrs. Caroline D. *Downright Dencey;* il. by M. W. Barney. Doubleday, 1927. Nantucket of a hundred years ago is the background for an impulsive, lovable, and very real little girl heroine. Ages 11–13.

Spring, Howard. *Tumbledown Dick, All People and No Plot;* with sixteen il. from pen drawings by Steven Spurrier. Viking, 1940. A book full of action, unexpected and entertaining happenings, and amusing and delightful characters. This is a book with the flavor of real literature, and Steven Spurrier's delightful drawings have the humor and liveliness of the text. Ages 11–15.

Streatfeild, Noel. *Circus Shoes;* il. in color by Richard Floethe. Random House, 1939. Life behind the scenes at the circus. The children of the story are real, and the events and setting are interesting. *Theatre Shoes,* il. by Richard Floethe (Random House, 1945), tells of two sisters and a brother who come to London during the war to live with their grandmother and attend a school for stage training. *Ballet Shoes,* il. by Richard Floethe (Random House, 1937), is the story of three children who lived in London and attended the Academy of Dancing and Stage Training. Ages 10–13.

Tarkington, Booth. *Penrod, His Complete Story.* Doubleday, 1914. This American boy, his dog, his friends, and his family are very real and much enjoyed by both boys and girls. Ages 12–14.

Torrey, Marjorie. *Penny;* il. by the author. Farrar, 1944. The friendships made by a shy little girl when she went to spend the summer with Great-aunt Penelope. Ages 7–10.

Tousey, Sanford. *Lumberjack Bill.* Houghton, 1943. The story of young Bill's visit to a lumber camp, where he learns to walk the moving logs and to make himself useful to the men in many ways, moves swiftly and is full of actuality and authentic details. Ages 7–11.

Trent, Bobbie. *Susan;* il. by Esther Waite. Viking, 1944. This little girl in Kentucky, fifty years ago, is so alive, so full of personality, that we follow her childish experiences as though she were someone we knew today. A background of fine family understanding. Ages 8–11.

Tunis, John R. *All-American;* il. by Hans Walleen. Harcourt, 1942. A football story with speed and suspense that touches also on the issue and values underlying the life of any American high school. Ages 10–14.

Tunis, John R. *Iron Duke;* il. by Johan Bull. Harcourt, 1938. A college story of today with Harvard as a setting. Unusually good characterization. Ages 12–15.

Turnbull, Agnes Sligh. *Elijah the Fishbite;* il. by Meg Wohlberg. Macmillan, 1940. Beginning with the incident of a kitten who ventured into church during Sunday morning service (the sermon that Sunday was about Elijah), to be removed hastily and with great presence of mind by Jimmie, the minister's youngest son, this is a chronicle of the lively doings of a family of boys and girls. A fine and understanding relationship between parents and children is suggested. Ages 9–11.

Twain, Mark. *Adventures of Tom Sawyer.* Harper, 1875–1938. *Adventures of Huckleberry Finn.* Harper, 1884–1912. Two classics of boyhood that hold their own. *Tom Sawyer* is based on reminiscences of the author's life in Missouri; in the second, "Huck" Finn, his dog, and his friend Negro Jim happily drift down the Mississippi River in search of adventure. Ages 11–14.

Urmston, Mary. *The Mystery of the Old Barn;* il. by Grace Paull. Doubleday, 1945. A well-constructed plot, a not-incredible mystery, natural lively children, and fine family relationships characterize this story. Ages 9–12.

Van Stockum, Hilda. *The Mitchells;* il. by the author. Viking, 1945. The exciting wartime summer of a large lively family and what happened when Father went to join his ship, leaving Mother, Grannie, Joan, Betsy, Peter, Angela, and Baby Timmy to carry on. Ages 9–12.

Wells, Rhea. *An American Farm;* il. by the author. Doubleday, 1928. In this story of two boys on a Tennessee farm, the author supplies a graphic, detailed account of a way of life with which few children of today are familiar. Ages 9–12.

White, Eliza Orne. *Training Sylvia;* il. by Dorothy Bayley. Houghton, 1942. Sylvia, aged nine, comes from Europe, where she has spent most of her short life, to stay with her New England relatives. Miss White, with understanding and a delightful humor, shows us a natural, impulsive, and very human little girl, whose own happy nature reacted happily on a somewhat staid household, where the adults were, however, intelligent and comprehending. *Where Is Adelaide?*, il. by Helen Sewell (Houghton, 1933); *Lending Mary,* il. by Grace Paull (Houghton, 1934); and *When Esther Was a Little Girl,* il. by Connie Moran (Houghton, 1944), are only three other titles of many books about little girls which this author has written with unfailing understanding and humor. Ages 9–12.

Wiggin, Kate Douglas. *Rebecca of Sunnybrook Farm;* il. by H. M. Grose. Houghton, 1925. (Riverside Bookshelf.) First published in 1903. Rebecca is a very real, impulsive, and endearing little heroine, still contemporary in feeling with children of today. Ages 10–14.

Wilder, Mrs. Laura I. *Little House in the Big Woods;* il. by Helen Sewell. Harper, 1932. The first of a series of seven books based on the author's own experiences in the pioneer West. The authentic background, sensitive characterization, and fine integrity make these invaluable as a genuine picture of American life. The other titles, all published by Harper, are *Farmer Boy* (1933); *Little Town on the Prairie* (1941); *On the Banks of Plum Creek* (1937); *By the Shores of Silver Lake* (1939); *The Long Winter* (1940); *These Happy Golden Years* (1943). Ages 8–14.

Worth, Kathryn. *The Middle Button;* il. by Dorothy Bayley. Doubleday, 1941. It was not so easy for girls to enter a profession in the 1880's as it is today, and when Maggie McArn, at thirteen, announced her intention of becoming a doctor, her family was both shocked and amused. Maggie's Scotch spunk, however, saw her through. A good story and a fine portrait of a very human girl. Ages 12–14.

CHAPTER XLI

Boys and Girls of Other Lands

To READ about boys and girls in other countries not only shows us how people live in different parts of the world, but makes us realize how much, in spite of different ways and different speech, we have in common.

Alessios, Alison Baigrie. *The Spear of Ulysses;* il. by Rafaello Busoni. Longmans, 1941. A story of modern Greece told with quiet charm. While she describes in interesting fashion the adventures of two boys who are searching for the spear of Ulysses, the author shows how the past has survived in the present and how old legends still play a part in the thought and lives of the Greeks of today. Ages 9–11.

Alger, Leclaire. *The Golden Summer;* pictures by Aldren Watson. Harper, 1942. The story of two children in a small Slovak village, one a shy sensitive boy, the ward of the village doctor, the other that same doctor's lively, mischievous niece. There is the ring of truth in this tale, which in spontaneous, unaffected fashion conveys something of the charm and simplicity of Slovak village life. Ages 9–12.

Angelo, Valenti. *Nino;* il. by the author. Viking, 1938. The author tells of his own life in a Tuscan village, with an artist's eye and an artist's memory for all the details—gracious, humorous, lively or serious—of those early years. There are friendly human relationships and plenty of fun and lively adventures which boys and girls will enjoy. *Golden Gate,* il. by the author (Viking, 1939), tells how Nino came to America to join his father and describes sympathetically the adjustments, excitements, and adventures of making a new home in a new land. *Paradise Valley,* il. with lithographs by the author (Viking, 1940), tells of a little

Mexican boy who came to live in an old caboose looking out over the Nevada desert, giving a picture of family life that belongs both to Mexico and the United States. Ages 9–12.

Arason, Steingrimur. *Smoky Bay: The Story of a Small Boy in Iceland;* il. by Gertrude Howe. Macmillan, 1942. The story of a very real small boy who obtains his dearest wish, cherished in secret, which was to visit America. The author, who is an Icelander, has drawn an authentic picture of an interesting country. *Golden Hair,* il. by Gertrude Howe, by the same author (Macmillan, 1945), tells of a visit a little girl from Dakota makes to her relatives in Iceland, describing many Icelandic customs, both old and new. Ages 9–12.

Armer, Laura Adams. *Forest Pool;* pictures by the author. Longmans, 1938. This story of two little boys who seek and find the iguana, the "wise old one," hoping he will tell them the secret they long to know, has caught in its beautiful pictures and simple childlike text, the feeling of golden sunshine and leisurely Mexican days. Ages 7–9.

Ayscough, Florence Wheelock. *Firecracker Land;* il. by Lucille Douglass. Houghton, 1932. The author, who has lived many years in China, writes sympathetically of the customs and the culture of the vanished China of the past. Ages 12–15.

Bartusek, Libushka. *Happy Times in Czechoslovakia;* foreword by Eleanor Roosevelt; drawings by Yarka Bures. Knopf, 1940. The author describes the everyday doings of a country family, telling of customs and festivals; and, with the help of the brightly colored illustrations full of peasant design, gives an authentic feeling of Czechoslovakian life. Ages 9–10.

Bemelmans, Ludwig. *Hansi;* il. by the author. Viking, 1934. Mr. Bemelmans' large, full-page pictures in color and lively, spontaneous story present imaginatively a little boy's Christmas holiday visit to his uncle in a village high up in the mountains of the Austrian Tirol. Ages 6–8. In *The Golden Basket,* il. by the author (Viking, 1936), Mr. Bemelmans recounts the adventures of two little English girls during a winter spent in Bruges, with that charming city made very vivid by the many lovely pictures. Ages 7–10.

Bennett, Richard. *Shawneen and the Gander*. Doubleday, 1937. An amusing story, with folk-tale flavor, about a little boy who meets a leprechaun. Ages 7–9.

Best, Herbert. *Garram the Hunter: A Boy of the Hill Tribes;* il. by Erick Berry. Doubleday, 1930. In this story of an African boy from the hills and his wonderful dog, the author, who has lived among the people he describes, gives a good picture of the country and of African life seen from the native point of view. The adventures of Garram, told here with humor and sympathy, are exciting. Ages 10–14.

Blackstock, Josephine. *Island on the Beam*. Putnam, 1944. A spirited story of Malta's struggle against invasion in the Second World War, as seen through the eyes of four children. Shows the courage, devotion, and unity with which the island met the invasion when it came. Ages 9–12.

Brock, Emma L. *At Midsummer Time: A Story of Sweden*. Knopf, 1940. This story of the celebration of Midsummer Eve and a little girl's enjoyment of the festival, gives us, in text and drawings, the atmosphere of another country and a picture of childhood that is true and gay and gracious. Ages 9–10.

Buff, Mary and Conrad. *Kobi: A Boy of Switzerland;* lithographs by Conrad Buff. Viking, 1940. Mr. Buff, who is a native of Appenzell, in his many beautiful full-page and double-page pictures and black and white drawings, seems to open wide a window on the Swiss mountain country. The story of sturdy nine-year-old Kobi tells of everyday things in the life of the Swiss mountaineers—milking and haying, cheese making, singing and yodeling, and evenings on the high Alps. Ages 9–11.

Burglon, Nora. *Children of the Soil; a Story of Scandinavia;* il. by E. P. d'Aulaire. Doubleday, 1932. Two Swedish children who, in spite of poverty, managed to live a happy, interesting life and to obtain through their efforts the cow, chickens, and ducks that they wanted. The author's *Sticks Across the Chimney; a Story of Denmark,* il. by Fritz Eichenberg (Holiday House, 1938), is a lively story of two children who live with their mother on a farm near an old Viking mound. There is a thread of mystery connected with the mound, and the characters are real. Ages 9–11.

Busoni, Rafaello. *Somi Builds a Church, a Story from Lapland;* il. by the author. Viking, 1943. The true story of how, with great labor and sacrifice, a church was built of logs in a land where no trees grew. The author knows and respects the Lapp character. Ages 10–11.

Collin, Hedvig. *Wind Island;* il. by the author. Viking, 1945. The story tells how a fisherman's children managed to make a beautiful amber necklace for their mother's birthday. The many lovely drawings and the artist-author's graphic style, make this tiny, charming island off the coast of Denmark very real to the reader. Ages 8–12.

Dalgliesh, Alice. *Little Angel;* il. by Katherine Milhous. Scribner, 1943. Gay, warm-hearted story of the Silva family of Rio, Brazil, and especially of Maria da Gloria, who was, for one day, an "angel" in a church procession. Ages 9–11.

D'Aulaire, Ingri and Edgar Parin. *Ola.* Doubleday, 1932. A beautiful, large picture book of Norway. The childlike, interesting text and the lithographic drawings in color and in black and white, tell of the adventures of a little Norwegian boy. *Ola and Blakken* (Doubleday, 1933) tells more about Ola and his little sisters; *Children of the Northlights* (Doubleday, 1935), in distinguished and beautiful pictures and clear, simple text, describes a year in the life of two children in Lapland. Ages 6–9.

Davis, Robert. *Pepperfoot of Thursday Market;* il. by Cyrus LeRoy Baldridge. Holiday House, 1941. Pepperfoot is a donkey saved from the jackals by Driss, a boy of the Berber tribes in the high Atlas Mountains of North Africa. In describing the adventures of Driss and the engaging and intelligent Pepperfoot, the author, who knows the Berbers at first hand, has written a vivid, convincing, and adventurous tale, which gives an excellent picture of a little-known country and the brave and simple people who live there. Ages 9–12.

De Jong, Dola. *The Level Land;* il. by Jan Hoowij. Scribner, 1944. This story of a Dutch family before and during the German invasion is full of the strength, humor, and dignity with which a courageous people faced and rose above the tragedy of war and occupation. Ages 9–12.

Dodge, Mary Mapes. *Hans Brinker; or, The Silver Skates;* il. by G. W. Edwards. Scribner, 1915. (Scribner Illustrated Classics.) First published in 1865. Written long ago and accepted in Holland as a true picture of Dutch child life, Mrs. Dodge's tale is still read and loved, for her characters have a reality which children everywhere find convincing. Ages 9–12.

Elliot, Kathleen Morrow. *Riema, Little Brown Girl of Java;* il. by Roger Duvoisin. Knopf, 1937. Sympathetic picture of life in Java, with a story that appeals to little girls. The author's *Soomoon, Boy of Bali,* il. by Roger Duvoisin (Knopf, 1938), relates the adventures of a mischievous ten-year-old on the island of Bali. The pictures in both books are brilliant in color and enhance the atmosphere of the tales. Ages 9–12.

Flexner, Hortense. *The Wishing Window;* drawings by Wyncie King. Stokes, 1942. A childlike, natural little story of two children in a French village in wartime who play a wishing game about a bakeshop window, and whose wishes, strangely enough, come true. Without harrowing the feelings of child readers in America, it will give them an idea of what has happened to other less fortunate children. Ages 7–11.

Foster, Elizabeth. *Gigi; the Story of a Merry-Go-Round Horse;* il. by Ilse Bischoff. Houghton, 1943. The story of a merry-go-round horse whose travels brought him from the Wurstelprater in Vienna to France, England, and finally America. Gigi, who is made more real by the distinguished drawings which heighten the Old World atmosphere of the book, is very appealing to boys and girls, who find the gracious, happy ending of the tale entirely satisfying. Ages 8–11.

French, Henry Willard. *The Lance of Kanana, a Story of Arabia in the Fourth Century;* il. by Wilfred Jones. Lothrop, 1932. A stirring story of a Bedouin boy who gave his life for his country. Ages 10–12.

Gatti, Attilio. *Saranga: The Pygmy;* il. by Kurt Wiese. Scribner, 1939. An authentic story of the life of a pygmy boy in the equatorial jungle of Africa. Ages 10–14.

Gay, Zhenya and Crespi, Pachita. *Manuelito of Costa Rica.* Messner, 1940. The simple text and Zhenya Gay's delightful pictures, brilliant in color and full of atmosphere, make an interesting country very real to boys and girls. Ages 6–8.

Gill, Richard C. *Manga; an Amazon Jungle Indian;* il. by H. M. Stoops. Stokes, 1937. A scientist, who has lived in the country of which he writes, tells the story of an Indian boy of Ecuador, his friendship with a young American photographer, and their adventures in the territory of the head-hunters, with a background of tribal customs. Ages 11–14.

Hamsun, Fru Marie Andersen. *A Norwegian Farm;* abridged and trans. by M. C. Darnton; il. by Elsa Jemne. Lippincott, 1934. This tells us of a very real family of brothers and sisters who are droll, honest, and unexpected. There is a fine background of outdoor living. Ages 10–13.

Hogeboom, Amy. *Gay Kilties of Cape Breton;* written and il. by Amy Hogeboom. Dutton, 1941. A lively tale of the daily doings of boys and girls on Cape Breton Island, in Nova Scotia. The occupations and industries, the history and legends of the country are woven easily and naturally into the story. Ages 9–12.

Hudson, William H. *A Little Boy Lost;* il. by Dorothy Lathrop. Knopf, 1920. In this beautifully written story of a little boy in South America who loses himself in the pursuit of a mirage, the naturalist-author expresses his own delight as a child in exploring wild, lonely places. Ages 11–13.

Jones, Idwal. *Whistler's Van;* il. by Zhenya Gay. Viking, 1936. This tale of the gypsies in Wales, written from firsthand knowledge, makes the reader free in a country whose charm and beauty have remained unchanged from the time of the Druids. Ages 11–14.

Lattimore, Eleanor Frances. *Little Pear, the Story of a Little Chinese Boy.* Harcourt, 1931. The everyday adventures of a little Chinese boy, told with charm and sincerity. Followed by *Little Pear and His Friends.* Harcourt, 1934. The author's own engaging drawings help to make her characters very real. *Peachblossom,* il. by the author (Harcourt, 1943), is the story, by an author who knows China well, of a little Chinese girl caught in the midst of the war. Ages 7–9.

Laverty, Maura. *Gold of Glanaree;* il. by Betty Morgan Bowen. Longmans, 1945. Happy child life in a delightful Irish family against a background of bog and hill, purple heather, and cowslip-sprinkled meadow. There are plenty of incidents and activities to hold the interest, and in particular a hunt for long-forgotten treasure undertaken by the children after they have heard mysterious sounds coming from the old fort of Glanaree. Ages 9–12.

Levy, Harry. *The Bombero; Tales from Latin America;* drawings by Howard Simon. Knopf, 1943. Four natural, childlike tales of children in Guayaquil, Mexico, Argentina, and Peru. Ages 7–10.

Lewis, Elizabeth Foreman. *Young Fu of the Upper Yangtze;* il. by Kurt Wiese. Winston, 1932. Accurate, vivid, and well-written story of modern China. The author's *Ho-Ming, Girl of New China,* il. by Kurt Wiese (Winston, 1934), suggests the conflict between the old and the new, and her *When the Typhoon Blows,* il. by Kurt Wiese (Winston, 1942), is a spirited story of the Japanese invasion of China. Ages 11–14.

Miller, Elizabeth Cleveland. *Children of the Mountain Eagle;* il. by Maud and Miska Petersham. Doubleday, 1927. Well-written, interesting story of Albanian children which makes the primitive life and customs of these mountain people, and the mountains themselves, very real. Ages 10–12.

Mirza, Youel Benjamin. *Myself When Young, a Boy in Persia;* il. by Theodore Nadejen. Doubleday, 1929. The author describes his own boyhood with charm and grace. His *Children of the Housetops,* il. by Frank Dobias (Doubleday, 1931), is a spontaneous and authentic tale of a young girl in a small Persian village. Ages 10–14.

Perkins, Mrs. Lucy Fitch. *The Dutch Twins.* Houghton, 1911. A perennial favorite that deals, with fine simplicity, with everyday matters well within the young child's interest. The author's delightful drawings add to the charm of the book. Ages 6–10.

Petroff, Boris G. *Son of the Danube;* il. with fourteen woodcuts by Hans Alexander Mueller. Viking, 1940. The author has used his own boyhood to make an authentic background for the adventurous and sometimes mischievous doings of a group of likable, high-spirited, energetic boys. The fine woodcuts add to the atmosphere and quality of the book. Ages 10–13.

Pollock, Katherine. *Sandalio Goes to Town;* with il. by Rafaello Busoni. Scribner, 1942. The story of a little Chilean boy and his pet calf. The reader will learn many facts about Chile, but the author has woven them unobtrusively into the narrative without lessening the spontaneity and interest of the story. Ages 9–12.

Purdon, Eric. *The Valley of the Larks; a Story of Inner Mongolia;* il. by Graham Peck. Farrar, 1939. The author, who was a member of an expedition that took him for five months into the interior of Inner Mongolia by camel, has written a vivid tale involving the Altai Lama, describing the great Maidari festival, and giving a strong sense of the beauty and strangeness of the little known land north of the Yellow River. Graham Peck, who also knows this region, has made drawings which heighten the atmosphere of the tale. Ages 10–13.

Rosanov, Sergei. *The Adventures of Misha;* trans. from the Russian by Ivy Low; drawings by Alexander Mogilevsky. Stokes, 1938. Misha is separated from his father in the Moscow Railroad Station, and before they come together again, the reader, as well as Misha, learns about the operation of the telegraph, telephone, the railroad, newspaper, street car, and motor bus system. In addition to much information about the life of a big city, the story has lively, natural conversation, convincing characters, humor, and action. Ages 7–10.

Rowe, Dorothy. *Rabbit Lantern, and Other Stories of Chinese Children;* il. by Ling Jui Tang. Macmillan, 1925. Pleasing, understanding stories of Chinese boys and girls. Ages 7–10.

Sawyer, Ruth. *The Least One;* il. by Leo Politi. Viking, 1941. In this story of a little boy whose dearly loved burro was lost and restored to him, the author has used her firsthand knowledge to give us an authentic Mexican background and a picture of a real and endearing child. Leo Politi's delightful drawings deepen the atmosphere of the book. Ages 8–12.

Seidlin, Oskar and Rypins, Senta. *Green Wagons;* il. by Barbara Cooney. Houghton, 1943. The story of a traveling theater troupe in Switzerland; how, with the help of the children in the town, the mystery of the stolen Golden Apple, the town symbol, is solved. Gaiety and originality characterize the story. Ages 8–12.

Seredy, Kate. *The Good Master;* il. by the author. Viking, 1935. A lively, spontaneous tale of child life on a great ranch on the Hungarian plain. Based on the author's own childhood experience, it has integrity and a fine human quality. Followed by *The Singing Tree;* il. by the author. Viking, 1939. Ages 9–12.

Shannon, Monica. *Dobry;* il. by Atanas Katchamakoff. Viking, 1934. The story of a Bulgarian boy who wanted to become a sculptor. The author's style, vivid and rich in color, makes the Bulgarian land and the peasant people extraordinarily real. The illustrations, too, have power and beauty. Ages 10–13.

Shaw, Flora L. *Castle Blair;* il. by George Varian. Little, 1923. First published in 1877. Ireland has changed since this story of five Irish children was written, but young readers still find these boys and girls and their doings interesting because of the life and individuality which the author has given them. Ages 10–13.

Singh, R. Lal and Lownsbery, Eloise. *Gift of the Forest;* il. by Anne Vaughan. Longmans, 1942. A story of rural India in which Bim, a little village boy, finds a tiger cub, the gift of the jungle, cares for him, loves him, and finally, when his pet is grown, is reconciled to giving him back to the forest. Many sidelights on the customs and thought of the people. Anne Vaughan's drawings are accurate and beautiful. Ages 9–14.

Sperry, Armstrong. *Bamboo, the Grass Tree;* story and pictures by Armstrong Sperry. Macmillan, 1942. In describing the daily life of a little boy on the Yangtze by means of a simple story, the author explains the importance of bamboo and its many uses in Chinese life. The little hero is very convincing, and Mr. Sperry's pictures have beauty and atmosphere. *Coconut, the Wonder Tree,* story and pictures by Armstrong Sperry (Macmillan, 1942), is a similar tale of a little boy and the uses of the coconut palm in the South Sea Islands. Ages 6–10.

Sperry, Armstrong. *Call It Courage;* il. by the author. Macmillan, 1940. Based on a Polynesian legend, this tells of Mafatu, a chief's son who, born with a fear of the sea, determines to conquer his terror and goes away alone in his canoe, with only his dog and pet albatross. Mafatu's adventures, his resourcefulness in danger, his victory over himself, and his final triumphal return, make a strong and heroic tale. Mr. Sperry knows the South Seas, and his fine drawings have the same spirit of adventure and genuine atmosphere as the text. Ages 9–12.

Spyri, Johanna. *Heidi;* il. by Gustaf Tenggren. Houghton, 1923. (Riverside Bookshelf.) First published in 1880. The freshness and simplicity of this story of a little girl in the Swiss mountains has given it a lasting charm. Ages 8–11.

Steen, Elizabeth K. *Red Jungle Boy;* written and il. by Elizabeth K. Steen. Harcourt, 1937. The life of an Indian boy in the Brazilian jungle, how he learned to use a man's weapons and do a man's work, is described in a simple, interesting story, with large, colorful pictures. Ages 9–11.

Stevens, Alden Gifford. *Lion Boy, a Tale of East Africa;* drawings by E. A. Watson. Stokes, 1938. Episodes in the life of Simba, "Lion Boy" (so-called because his father was a great hunter), his family, and his tribe in a mud-walled village in Tanganyika. The author draws on memories of his personal experience, and writes with understanding and admiration for the native tribesmen. Ages 10–13.

Still, Dorris Shelton. *Sue in Tibet;* il. by William Arthur Smith. Day, 1942. Vivid story of a summer spent in Tibet by the lively and engaging young daughter of an American doctor who, granted permission from the High Lama to visit the country, takes his family with him. The picture of this remote corner of the world is accurate; the author lived in Tibet as a child and some of the experiences she describes were her own. Ages 10–14.

Tarshis, Elizabeth Kent. *The Village That Learned to Read;* il. by Harold Haydon. Houghton, 1941. The story of a Mexican village in which the establishment of the first school was to be celebrated by a fiesta when all the village had learned to read. Pedro, who wanted to be a bull-fighter and not a scholar, almost broke the record; and the efforts of the villagers to bring him into line make an amusing and human story. The setting is authentic and colorful. Ages 9–12.

Undset, Sigrid. *Happy Times in Norway;* trans. from the Norwegian by Joran Birkeland; decorations by Norman Reeves. Knopf, 1942. The story of this great writer's own home and family. The good times, the mischief, the family customs and festivals are described in vivid, zestful, humorous fashion, and without bitterness, though the book was written after the Germans entered Norway. Ages 9–12.

Van Stockum, Hilda. *Cottage at Bantry Bay;* il. by the author. Viking, 1938. Well characterized story of an Irish family of four lively children, against a background of one of the loveliest sections of Ireland. Ages 10–12.

Van Stockum, Hilda. *A Day on Skates, the Story of a Dutch Picnic.* Harper, 1934. The charming pictures in color and the lively text have a reality which makes the reader feel that he shares all the adventures of that long day in the open air, from the exhilaration of the start, to the comforting warmth of the sledge that gives them a lift home, and the lamplit welcome. Ages 8–10.

Waldeck, Jo Besse McElveen. *Little Jungle Village;* il. by Katharine von Dombrowski. Viking, 1940. Author and illustrator know the South American jungle at first hand, and this story of a native eleven-year-old boy and his younger sister is told with reality and distinction. Ages 9–12.

Wells, Rhea. *Ali the Camel; a Story of North Africa.* Doubleday, 1931. North Africa supplies the background for this story of a camel with a well-developed personality. The decorations in black and white are characteristic of the art of the country, and the illustrations in color show authentic costumes and typical scenes. *Beppo the Donkey,* a story of Sicily (Doubleday, 1930), is an attractive book about Sicily by the same author. *Coco the Goat* (Doubleday, 1929), the story of a mischievous baby goat, is written with an authentic Spanish setting. Ages 7–9.

Williams, Henry Lionel. *Kimbi, Jungle Indian;* il. by Harry Daugherty. Random House, 1942. (Children of the Americas.) The author, who has a firsthand knowledge of the Jivaros Indians, famous for shrinking the heads of enemies captured in battle, tells a swiftly moving tale of a boy of the tribe who, in order to save his pet monkey from the cooking pot, borrows his grandfather's blowpipe and poisoned darts to add to the food supply and shows so much bravery and skill that he wins the rank of hunter and a man's weapons for his own. Ages 8–10.

Wood, Esther. *Silk and Satin Lane;* il. by Kurt Wiese. Longmans, 1939. The story of an impulsive little Chinese girl whose good intentions and honest, affectionate nature win her a place in the heart and home of her wood-carver uncle in the ancient city of Chaohing. The story has caught the atmosphere of China and the friendliness and humor of the people. Ages 9–11.

CHAPTER XLII

Stories of Adventure

ALL of us are adventurers at heart, and with the power to travel that books place at our disposal, there is no enterprise we may not share, no remote part of the universe we may not visit.

Ames, Merlin M. *Canthook Country;* il. by Harvey Kidder. Houghton, 1941. A tale of the lumber camps of the Northwest in which the hero, Steve Adams, learns to swing an axe and use a "canthook." Sharing day by day in the hard, dangerous work of a lumberjack, he grows up and becomes a man whose strength and courage do not fail him in a final test provided by a forest fire. A book with a fine integrity and clarity of vision. Ages 12–15.

Baker, Elizabeth W. *Stocky, Boy of West Texas;* il. by Charles Hargens, Winston, 1945. A likable boy of fifteen is the hero of this story of Comanche Indians, cattle-rustlers, rattlesnakes, and bobcats, which provides a very real picture of Texas in its early days. Ages 10–15.

Bell, Margaret. *The Pirates of Icy Strait;* il. by Harvey Kidder. Morrow, 1943. A tale, packed with adventure but never overdrawn, of the Alaska fishing industry, with an authentic geographic background. *Danger on Old Baldy,* il. by Hamilton Greene (Morrow, 1944), and *Enemies in Icy Strait,* il. by George M. Richards (Morrow, 1945), tell of further adventures of the same characters. Ages 11–15.

Buchan, John. *The Thirty-Nine Steps.* Houghton, 1915. An absorbing adventure story, dealing with the British Intelligence service before and during the first European war, and written with a zest and imaginative power that make the reader feel he shares in the events of the book. *Greenmantle* (Houghton, 1916), and *Mr. Standfast* (Houghton, 1919), continue the adventures of Richard Hannay, the hero. Ages 12–15.

Chapman, Maristan. *Wild Cat Ridge;* il. by J. C. McKell. Appleton-Century, 1932. There is a spirit of adventure and real boy characters in this authentic, present-day story of the Tennessee mountain country. Followed by *Timber Trail* (Appleton-Century, 1933), and *Eagle Cliff* (Appleton-Century, 1934). Ages 10–13.

Davis, Robert. *Hudson Bay Express;* il. by Henry Pitz. Holiday House, 1942. A spirited tale of dog teams in the eastern Canadian wilderness of James Bay, full of exciting adventure for two boys, one white and one Indian, who organized a dog freight- and passenger-line. Much authentic information about dog teams and sledging. Ages 11–15.

Dean, Graham M. *Riders of the Gabilans.* Viking, 1944. A story about cowboys, horses, and ranch life, round-ups, range riding, and the outwitting of cattle thieves; vigorous, vivid, and authentic. Ages 9–14.

Defoe, Daniel. *Robinson Crusoe;* il. by E. B. Smith. Houghton, 1909. (Riverside Bookshelf.) This story of a shipwrecked sailor who lived alone on a desert island for twenty-eight years is one of the supreme adventure stories of all time. Ages 10–14.

Desmond, Alice Curtis. *The Sea Cats;* il. by Wilfrid Bronson. Macmillan, 1944. This well-told adventure story of the Pribilof Islands gives much fascinating information about the habits of seals and the way in which the government, with the aid of Aleut sailors, protects them. Ages 9–12.

Doyle, Sir A. Conan. *The Boys' Sherlock Holmes;* arr. by Howard Haycraft; il. with photographs. Harper, 1936. Twelve of the famous cases solved by the great detective and his friend, Dr. Watson. Ages 10–14.

Edmonds, Walter D. *Wilderness Clearing;* il. by John S. de Martelly. Dodd, 1944. A story of the American Revolution as it affected the settlers in the Mohawk Valley. Told with drama and suspense and a thread of romance. Ages 12–15.

Haig-Brown, Roderick L. *Starbuck Valley Winter;* il. by Charles DeFeo. Morrow, 1943. A winter spent by a sixteen-year-old boy trapping marten in an unexplored valley in British Columbia. Lively adventure, characters that come to life, and a fine outdoor atmosphere. Ages 10–15.

Household, Geoffrey. *The Spanish Cave;* with il. by Henry C. Pitz. Little, 1936. A swiftly moving adventure story, with the native superstition and romantic mystery of a Spanish coast village as a background. Ages 12–14.

Kipling, Rudyard. *Kim.* Doubleday, 1901. Kipling's famous story is an open sesame to the color and romance and adventure of the nineteenth-century India which the author knew so well. Ages 12–15.

Kjelgaard, Jim. *Forest Patrol;* il. by Tony Palazzo. Holiday House, 1941. An excellent story, fresh and unhackneyed in setting and incident, with characters that convince and genuine outdoor atmosphere. The book throws light on the purpose and methods of conservation and provides a fine picture of a profession that should appeal to many boys. Ages 12–14.

Marryat, Frederick. *Children of the New Forest;* ed. by May McNeer; il. by Lynd Ward. Macmillan, 1930. (Children's Classics.) First published in 1846. This old tale of four orphaned children at the time of the English Civil War, who are hidden by a keeper in the New Forest and brought up as his grandchildren, still holds excitement and interest. Ages 11–14.

Masefield, John. *Jim Davis;* with eight il. in color by Mead Schaeffer. Stokes, 1924. Stirring tale of smugglers on the Devonshire coast, told with vigor and spontaneity. Ages 10–14.

Meader, Stephen W. *Shadow in the Pines;* il. by Edward Shenton. Harcourt, 1942. The scene is laid in the New Jersey pine barrens, where the fifteen-year-old hero helps round up a gang of Nazi Fifth Columnists who are threatening the safety of Fort Dix. Ages 11–15.

Meader, Stephen W. *Who Rides in the Dark?;* il. by James MacDonald. Harcourt, 1937. A lively tale of the adventures of fifteen-year-old Daniel Drew of Portsmouth, with a fine flavor of early New Hampshire in days just after the War of 1812. Ages 12–14.

Newcomb, Covelle. *Silver Saddles;* il. by Addison Burbank. Longmans, 1943. A swiftly moving story of a boy and a horse in Mexico. Ages 11–13.

Nordhoff, Charles B. and Hall, James N. *Falcons of France, a Tale of Youth and the Air;* il. by A. Vimnèra. Little, 1929. A young American's adventures with the Lafayette Flying Corps during the First World War. The authors lived through many of the experiences described and write with vividness and understanding. Ages 11–15.

Norton, André. *The Sword Is Drawn;* il. by Duncan Coburn. Houghton, 1944. Well-written story of a Dutch boy and how he served his country in the Second World War. Ages 10–15.

Page, Thomas Nelson. *Two Little Confederates;* il. by J. W. Thomason. Scribner, 1891. A convincing and very human little story of the adventures of two small boys with Union and Confederate soldiers during the Civil War. Ages 9–12.

Philbrook, Elizabeth. *Far from Marlborough Street.* Viking, 1944. A story packed full of excitement about a spirited little girl who traveled alone by stage coach from Boston to Springfield on a mission of importance. Ages 9–12.

Poe, Edgar Allan. *The Gold Bug and Other Tales and Poems.* Macmillan, 1930. (Children's Classics.) The mystery, strangeness, and beauty of these tales and poems is something no boy or girl should miss. Ages 12–15.

Skidmore, Hubert. *River Rising!;* il. by Benton Spruance. Doubleday, 1939. A story full of action and suspense, set in the North Carolina mountain country which the author knows well. York Allen's struggle to become a doctor, and his ambition to return and help the mountain communities, carries a fine suggestion of spirit of service and of courageous purpose. *Hill Doctor,* il. by Benton Spruance (Doubleday, 1940), tells of York Allen's return from medical school to practice among the Blue Ridge mountaineers. Ages 12–15.

Stevenson, Robert Louis. *Kidnapped, Being Memoirs of the Adventures of David Balfour in the Year 1751;* il. by N. C. Wyeth. Scribner, 1924. (Scribner Illustrated Classics.) Vivid, exciting, adventure story, the scene laid in Scotland shortly after the rising in support of Prince Charlie in 1745. The hero is kidnaped and cast away on a desert island; later he journeys to the Highlands, where he meets Alan Breck Stewart and other Highland followers of the Stuarts. David finally triumphs over his so-called uncle who had schemed for his downfall. Ages 12–15.

Wells, H. G. *Seven Famous Novels;* with a preface by the author. Knopf, 1941. Containing: "The Time Machine"; "Island of Dr. Moreau"; "Invisible Man"; "War of the Worlds"; "First Men in the Moon"; "Food of the Gods"; "In the Days of the Comet." These scientific romances, with their plausible detail and breathless adventure, delight both boys and their fathers. Ages 12–15.

Weston, Christine. *Bhimsa the Dancing Bear;* il. by Roger Duvoisin. Scribner, 1945. With intimate knowledge of India and imaginative perception the author tells an absorbing tale of two boys, David and Gopala, and their journey from the plains to the mountains, accompanied by Bhimsa, who, as Gopala says, "is an unusual bear, there is very little he doesn't understand and very little he can't do." Here is all the wonder of adventure, though the author stops just short of fantasy. India becomes very real in this book, which is written with beauty and distinction. Ages 8–12.

Wyss, Johann David. *Swiss Family Robinson;* ed. by G. E. Mitton; il. by Harry Rountree. Macmillan, 1924. (Children's Classics.) First appeared in Zurich in 1813. The resourceful housekeeping of this Swiss family shipwrecked on a desert island has charmed generations of children. It can be read earlier than Robinson Crusoe. Ages 9–12.

CHAPTER XLIII

Stories with an Historical Background

Altsheler, Joseph. *Young Trailers; a Story of Early Kentucky*. Appleton-Century, 1907. A story of pioneer life, hunting, and Indian fighting. The hero is one of the early settlers of what was afterward Kentucky. The author has written many other popular books with a background of American history. Ages 9–13.

Bennett, John. *Barnaby Lee*. Appleton-Century, 1902. This story of an English boy forced to serve on a pirate ship makes the days when Governor Peter Stuyvesant stumped about New Amsterdam on his wooden leg, and gallant Charles Calvert was governor in Maryland, very real. Ages 11–14.

Bennett, John. *Master Skylark; a Story of Shakespeare's Time;* il. by Reginald B. Birch. Appleton-Century, 1897. The story of a Stratford boy who runs away and joins a company of players. A well-written book full of admirable detail and atmosphere. Queen Elizabeth and Shakespeare are characters in the story. Ages 11–14.

Berry, Erick. *Harvest of the Hudson;* il. by the author. Macmillan, 1945. Fine story of a brother and sister in the days of the patroons. It includes the solving of a mystery and a voyage to the West Indies where the boy encounters pirates, shipwreck, and other adventures. Ages 10–13.

Best, Herbert. *Border Iron;* il. by Erick Berry. Viking, 1945. Sturdy, courageous Tod Randall and his dog help solve a border dispute over iron ore from Massachusetts for a furnace in New York Province in the 1750's. A good story against a background accurate in local color and historical detail. Ages 12–15.

Boyd, James. *Drums;* il. by N. C. Wyeth. Scribner, 1928. A stirring story of North Carolina in the early stages of the Revolution. Ages 12–15.

Boyd, Thomas. *Shadow of the Long Knives.* Peter Smith, 1935. A story of Ohio in Revolutionary days, seen through the eyes of Angus McDermott, Indian scout for the British. Ages 13–15.

Brink, Mrs. Carol Ryrie. *Caddie Woodlawn;* il. by Kate Seredy. Macmillan, 1935. The lively doings of Caddie and her two brothers in their home on the Wisconsin frontier in 1864. *Magical Melons,* il. by Marguerite Davis. Macmillan, 1944. Further adventures of Caddie and her brothers. Like the first volume, this has a fine flavor of pioneer life. Ages 9–12.

Chambers, Robert W. *Cardigan;* il. by Henry Pitz. Harper, 1930. Michael Cardigan, the hero, carries a message from Sir William Johnson to the Indians near Fort Pitt and finds himself involved in unexpected and dangerous adventures. The story ends with the battle of Lexington and Concord, in which Michael joins the Minutemen. Ages 12–14.

Coatsworth, Elizabeth. *Dancing Tom;* pictures by Grace Paull. Macmillan, 1938. This story of a family migration by flatboat, down the Mississippi a hundred years ago, has a real flavor of the period, though the style is simple enough for beginners to read by themselves. Ages 7–9.

Coatsworth, Elizabeth. *Sword of the Wilderness;* il. by Hervé Stein. Macmillan, 1936. A beautifully written story of Maine colonists and Indians in the French and Indian Wars, significant because it keeps the contrast between Indian and settler, explaining the inevitable conflict. Ages 11–14.

Cooper, James Fenimore. *The Deerslayer;* il. by N. C. Wyeth. Scribner, 1925. (Scribner's Illustrated Classics.) First published in 1841. This, with *The Last of the Mohicans* and *The Pathfinder,* are the three best stories in a series called *The Leatherstocking Tales,* which tells of Indian warfare and frontier life in New York State in the eighteenth century. Hawkeye, the Scout, and his Indian friends, Chingachgook and Uncas, are the leading characters. Ages 12–14.

Cormack, Maribelle and Alexander, William P. *Last Clash of the Claymores: A Story of Scotland in the Time of Prince Charles.* Appleton-Century, 1940. The events of this story cover the years 1744–46, when the hero meets Prince Charlie Stuart in France, accompanies him to Scotland, and remains with him during his first success and later when the Prince is a hunted fugitive. Dramatic and stirring, with the battle scenes very well done. Ages 12–14.

Crawford, Phyllis. *Hello, the Boat!;* pictures by Edward Laning. Holt, 1938. A story of the "westward movement," telling how a whole family, in 1817, went down the Ohio in a "storeboat" loaded with drygoods, pots, pans, and "Yankee notions." Ages 9–12.

Daniel, Hawthorne. *Shadow of the Sword;* il. by E. A. Verpilleux. Macmillan, 1930. A tale of France in the fifteenth century. Mont-Saint-Michel supplies a romantic setting, and the atmosphere is well-sustained. Ages 11–14.

Davis, Julia. *No Other White Men;* maps by Caroline Gray. Dutton, 1937. A stirring chronicle of the Lewis and Clark expedition. The author follows closely the diaries kept by the two leaders. Ages 12–14.

Dix, Beulah Marie. *Merrylips;* il. by F. T. Merrill and Anne Cooper; new ed. Macmillan, 1925. A lively story of the Cavaliers and Roundheads. The heroine escapes to the Cavalier army disguised as a boy. Ages 10–12.

Dix, Beulah Marie. *Soldier Rigdale;* il. by R. B. Birch. Macmillan, 1899. The story of a boy who came over in the *Mayflower,* was befriended by Miles Standish, and later saw much of life among the Indians. The background is accurate and the characters well-drawn. Ages 10–12.

Dumas, Alexandre. *Three Musketeers;* il. by Maurice Leloir. Dodd. First published 1844. (Great Illustrated Classics.) The dashing adventures of d'Artagnan, Athos, Porthos, and Aramis and the glamor of court life at Versailles under Louis XIV. Ages 12–15.

Field, Rachel Lyman. *Hitty; Her First Hundred Years;* il. by Dorothy Lathrop. Macmillan, 1929. Hitty, a wooden doll who writes her own memoirs, was carved from mountain ashwood by a peddler in Maine. There her adventures and journeys began, to continue for a century during which sturdy little Hitty was passed from hand to hand. The vivid, humorous text and the fine drawings give the reader a keen sense of the changes a hundred years have brought. Ages 10–12.

Forbes, Esther. *Johnny Tremain;* il. by Lynd Ward. Houghton, 1943. The Boston of 1774 is brilliantly recreated as a background for the hero, a sensitive, high-spirited boy who rapidly grows into maturity during the exciting years that preceded the Revolution. Ages 10–15.

Gray, Elizabeth Janet. *Beppy Marlowe of Charles Town;* il. by Loren Barton. Viking, 1936. Fine story of an interesting, natural girl. In the first half of the book, the background is eighteenth-century London, worked out with a fine regard for authentic detail; the scene of the second half is laid in "Charles Town," South Carolina. Ages 11–14.

Gray, Elizabeth Janet. *Meggy MacIntosh;* il. by Marguerite de Angeli. Doubleday, 1930. In 1775 a brave, fifteen-year-old Scotch girl ran away from Edinburgh, hoping to join the rescuer of Prince Charlie, Flora MacDonald, then living in North Carolina. Stirring adventure and vivid picture of the Scottish immigrants who came to North Carolina before the Revolution. Ages 11–14.

Grey, Katharine. *Rolling Wheels;* il. by Frank Schoonover. Little, 1937. (Beacon Hill Bookshelf.) The story of an Indiana family who, in 1845, took the overland route to California. Compiled from authentic accounts, the book is lifelike and vivid. Ages 11–13.

Hodges, C. Walter. *Columbus Sails;* with il. by the author. Coward-McCann, 1939. The author's fine vigorous drawings and the fresh quality of his imagination give new life and vividness to this well-known story. Ages 12–14.

Jewett, Eleanore Myers. *Told on the King's Highway;* il. by Marie A. Lawson. Viking, 1943. Sixteen tales of the Middle Ages retold with sympathy and affection. Marie Lawson's beautiful drawings play their part with the text in weaving a medieval tapestry where knights and ladies, churchmen, market women, men-at-arms, pilgrims, huntsmen, and country folk form a pageant of life long ago. Ages 9–12.

Johnston, Mary. *To Have and to Hold*. Houghton, 1931. Vivid picture of life in the early days of Virginia. It opens with the unloading of a ship-load of girls, sent from England to find husbands among the colonists. Ages 12–15.

Kelly, Eric P. *Trumpeter of Krakow, a Tale of the Fifteenth Century;* il. by Angela Pruszynska. Macmillan, 1928. A story of fifteenth-century Poland, full of local color and of details of life in a thrilling period. Ages 12–14.

Kent, Louise Andrews. *He Went with Christopher Columbus;* il. by Paul Quinn. Houghton, 1940. The likable young hero sails with Columbus on his famous voyage. The story is full of excitement and surprises, the background accurate, and Columbus himself is shown as a dignified and appealing figure. Ages 12–14.

King-Hall, Magdalen. *Sturdy Rogue;* il. by Addison Burbank. Winston, 1945. Lively adventures of a fourteen-year-old runaway who lived in Cornwall in Queen Elizabeth's reign. Authentic picture of the period with special emphasis on the Beggars' Brotherhood; a glossary of beggars' terms and cant is included. Ages 12–15.

Kipling, Rudyard. *Puck of Pook's Hill*. Doubleday, 1906. This and the author's *Rewards and Fairies* (Doubleday, 1910) combine an imaginative fairy tale with a masterly presentation of English history. The stories told to two children by "Puck" range in period from before the Norman Conquest to Napoleon. Ages 11–14.

Knox, Esther Melbourne. *Swift Flies the Falcon; a Story of the First Crusade;* il. by Ruth King. Winston, 1939. A Welsh brother and sister whose father is away fighting in the First Crusade, flee from their home to escape the plots of a treacherous uncle and manage to join their father in the East. A well-rounded picture of medieval life, full of color and picturesque detail. Ages 12–14.

Lide, Alice Alison. *Princess of Yucatan;* il. by Carlos Sanchez. Longmans, 1939. How a Mayan girl wins the freedom of her tribe after the city of Chichen Itza has fallen into the hands of the Aztec conquerors. A highly colored tale, based, however, on history. Ages 10–14.

Lownsbery, Eloise. *A Camel for a Throne;* il. by Elizabeth Tyler Wolcott. Houghton, 1941. Neferta, a princess of ancient Egypt, runs away to escape mistreatment at the hands of the royal nurse. A Nubian boy takes her across the desert on his camel, and together they journey on like nomads for a year, until ancient prophecies are proved true and Neferta is discovered to be not the niece, but the daughter of the Pharaoh. Ages 10–14.

Macdonald, Zillah K. *Flower of the Fortress.* Westminster Press, 1944. A story of the siege of Louisburg, in Cape Brêton in 1745, told in a fine vein of romantic adventure and with a wealth of authentic historical detail. Ages 11–14.

MacKaye, Loring and J. J. *We of Frabo Stand;* il. by Elsa Jemne. Longmans, 1944. This story of Gotland and the King of Denmark, full of medieval color, rich in humor and characterization, tells in stirring fashion of a country, betrayed, invaded, but undaunted, and of a boy and his goose who played a not unimportant part in crucial happenings. Ages 10–14.

McKown, Gretchen and Gleeson, F. S. *All the Days Were Antonia's;* il. by Zhenya Gay. Viking, 1939. The heroine goes west with her mother by stagecoach, in the 1870's, to Deadwood City, Dakota, where her father had already gone to establish a pioneer bank. The book has charm and humor, and the life of a mining town is made extraordinarily real. Ages 11–14.

Marsh, Janet. *Don't Tread on Me;* il. by Helen Torrey. Houghton, 1941. Ten well-told, dramatic tales ranging in period from prehistoric times to 1938, which illustrate the idea that democracy is not an abstract principle, but the give and take of freedom, hammered out as men learn to live together. Ages 10–13.

Marshall, Rosamond Van Der Zee. *None But the Brave;* il. by Gregor Duncan. Houghton, 1942. A spirited story of Holland in the sixteenth century during the siege of Leyden, when the Dutch were resisting a tyrant and struggling to win back the right to live in freedom. Ages 11–14.

Masefield, John. *Martin Hyde, the Duke's Messenger;* il. by T. C. Dugdale. Little, 1910. (Beacon Hill Bookshelf.) The author makes Martin, who takes part in Monmouth's rebellion in England in 1685, and the period itself, vivid and real. Ages 11–14.

Mayer, Albert I., Jr. *Falconer's Son;* il. by Sheilah Beckett. Westminster Press, 1941. A lively adventure story, with Central Europe, in the latter half of the tenth century when Charlemagne's empire had fallen to pieces, as a background. Full details that make life in the Middle Ages very real. Ages 11–14.

Mayer, Albert I., Jr. *Olympiad;* il. by Cleveland J. Woodward. Harper, 1938. A story of ancient Greece and a young athlete who attains his ambition to become champion of the "beardless" wrestlers at the Olympic Games. Boys will enjoy the detailed account of how an athlete in Greece received his training, how the games and contests were conducted, and the descriptions of wrestling matches. Ages 12–14.

Meader, Stephen W. *Boy with a Pack;* il. by Edward Shenton. Harcourt, 1939. Putting all his savings into a trunk full of "Yankee notions," Bill Crawford set out afoot from Connecticut for the Ohio country. Plenty of adventures, the difficulties of travel in 1837, and an authentic picture of this country a hundred years ago. Ages 11–14.

Meadowcroft, Mrs. Enid LaMonte. *By Wagon and Flatboat;* il. by Ninon MacKnight. Crowell, 1938. How two families in 1789 migrated from Pittsburgh to Losantiville, afterwards Cincinnati, journeying first by Conestoga wagon and then by flatboat. Ages 8–11.

Meadowcroft, Mrs. Enid LaMonte. *Ship Boy with Columbus;* il. by Jessie Robinson. Crowell, 1942. Boys and girls will not only enjoy the adventures of Pedro, the thirteen-year-old hero, but will find the picture which the author draws of the great Admiral stirring, comprehensible, and appealing. Ages 6–10.

Meadowcroft, Mrs. Enid LaMonte, *Silver for General Washington.* Crowell, 1944. An accurate, lively story that, as it describes how a brother and sister spent the winter at Valley Forge in the midst of General Washington's ragged, half-starved army, paints an impressive picture of the time, the courage and sheer deter-

mination of the soldiers, and the readiness of most of the townsfolk to co-operate. The children themselves find a way to help.
Ages 9–12.

Meigs, Cornelia. *Master Simon's Garden;* il. by John Rae. Macmillan, 1929. A picture of early America through three generations, beginning in the Puritan colony of Hopewell and ending
in Revolutionary times. Ages 11–14.

Meigs, Cornelia. *Willow Whistle;* il. by E. B. Smith. Macmillan,
1931. A thoroughly interesting story of pioneer days in the Middle West, telling of friendly Sioux Indians, of buffalo and Indian
ponies, and of the building of the first schoolhouse. Ages 7–11.

Neyhart, Louise A. *Henry's Lincoln;* il. by Charles Wilson Bank.
Holiday House, 1945. A little boy has his first big adventure
when he is allowed to drive Prince, the family horse, to town
by himself and represent the family at the Lincoln-Douglas De-
bate held in Freeport, Illinois, in 1858. The author makes Lincoln, his opponent, the audience of townspeople, and a memorable day very real. Ages 9–12.

Powers, Alfred. *Hannibal's Elephants;* il. by James Reid. Longmans, 1944. Agenor, keeper of elephants, tells the story of the
invasion of Italy in 216 B.C. with 100,000 warriors and thirty-
seven elephants. Ages 11–15.

Pyle, Howard. *Men of Iron.* Harper, 1891. Myles Falworth won
his spurs and overcame his own and his father's enemy in the
days of Henry IV. This swiftly moving tale gives a fine picture
of life in the great castles and of the training of a young knight
in England in the fourteenth century. Ages 10–14.

Pyle, Howard. *Otto of the Silver Hand.* Scribner, 1888. Beautifully
told tale of robber barons in medieval Germany. Ages 10–13.

Singmaster, Elsie. *A Boy at Gettysburg.* Houghton, 1924. A story
of the Civil War and the Underground Railway. The author's
Emmeline (Houghton, 1916) tells of the unexpectedly important role which fifteen-year-old Emmeline plays when some of
the rebel soldiers take refuge in her grandmother's house during
the Battle of Gettysburg. *Swords of Steel; the Story of a Gettysburg Boy,* il. by David Hendrickson (Houghton, 1933), gives a

graphic picture of the Battle of Gettysburg and also tells of incidents leading up to the struggle between the States. Ages 9–14.

Singmaster, Elsie. *Rifles for Washington;* with il. by Frank E. Schoonover. Houghton, 1938. Sixteen-year-old Davie McKail and his uncle, an old Indian fighter, both join Washington's troops. The story tells of their adventures during the war, ending in Yorktown. Ages 11–14.

Skinner, Constance Lindsay. *Silent Scot, Frontier Scout.* Macmillan, 1925. Story of the Tennessee border during the Revolutionary War. Other well-written and authentic books by this author dealing with frontier and pioneer life are: *The White Leader* (Macmillan, 1926); *Andy Breaks Trail* (Macmillan, 1928); *Rob Roy, the Frontier Twins* (Macmillan, 1934); *Becky Landers, Frontier Warrior* (Macmillan, 1926); *Debby Barnes, Trader* (Macmillan, 1932). Ages 11–14.

Snedeker, Mrs. Caroline D. *The Spartan.* Doubleday, 1912. In this story of the young hero who alone returned from the battle of Thermopylae, the author, with imaginative sympathy and a knowledge of sources, has brought to life a thrilling period in Greek history. Ages 12–15.

Snedeker, Mrs. Caroline D. *Uncharted Ways;* il. by M. deV. Lee. Doubleday, 1935. A novel for young people which paints a thoughtful picture of the Quakers in Puritan New England, in the seventeenth century. The heroine is drawn after Mary Dyer, one of the Quaker martyrs, but this story has a happy ending. Ages 12–15.

Snedeker, Mrs. Caroline D. *The White Isle;* il. by Fritz Kredel. Doubleday, 1940. The heroine, Lavinia, is the daughter of a patrician family exiled from Rome to Britain in the second century, A.D. The story combines a vivid picture of Roman life with the traditions of early Christianity. Ages 12–14.

Sperry, Armstrong. *Wagons Westward, the Old Trail to Santa Fe;* il. by the author. Winston, 1936. How a Missouri caravan crossed the plains in 1846 as it took the old trail to Santa Fe. Ages 11–14.

Steel, Flora A. *The Adventures of Akbar.* Stokes, 1913. The chief characters of this colorful book about the childhood of little

Prince Akbar, later a sixteenth-century Indian emperor, really lived. Ages 10–12.

Sutton, Margaret. *Jemima, Daughter of Daniel Boone;* il. by I. B. Hazelton. Scribner, 1942. A story of the great pioneer and his family, centering about Boone's youngest daughter, Jemima. The author follows history closely as she tells of the establishment of Fort Boonesborough and its gallant defense against the Indians. The book is full of details that make it a vivid picture of frontier life. Ages 11–14.

Swift, Mrs. Hildegarde Hoyt. *Railroad to Freedom; a Story of the Civil War;* il. by James Daugherty. Harcourt, 1932. In imaginary scenes, founded on fact, the author has skillfully told the story of Harriet Tubman, called the "Moses" of American slaves. Ages 12–15.

Twain, Mark. *The Prince and the Pauper;* il. by H. C. Pitz. Harper. First published in 1903. A dramatic story of how the boy King Edward VI and ragged Tom Canty exchanged clothes and places. Ages 11–13.

CHAPTER XLIV

Some Novels and Stories That Have Stood the Test of Time

SOME of these novels and tales were written a hundred years ago; some are even older; but their truth to human nature, their romance, adventure, and imagination have kept them alive for us today.

Aucassin and Nicolette; trans. by Andrew Lang; decorations by Maxwell Simpson. Holiday House, 1936. A song-story of the Middle Ages that tells in prose and verse, with a springtime loveliness, how two young lovers were separated and found one another again. Ages 12–15.

Austen, Jane. *Pride and Prejudice;* il. by C. E. and H. M. Brock. Macrae. (Rittenhouse Classics.) Written 1796–97. Jane Austen's stories have the full flavor of polite society in the eighteenth century. Her keen observation and her ability to describe people as she saw them give an absorbing interest to the characters and incidents of her novels. Those who enjoy *Pride and Prejudice* will want to read Miss Austen's other books: *Emma, Mansfield Park, Northanger Abbey, Persuasion, Sense and Sensibility,* which are published separately in Macmillan Illustrated Pocket Classics or as one volume in the Modern Library. Ages 12–15.

Barrie, Sir J. M. *The Little Minister.* Crowell. (Luxembourg Ed.) A swiftly moving tale of what happened in a quiet little Scottish village when the young minister of the kirk fell in love with a gypsy girl. Ages 12–15.

Swift, Jonathan. *Gulliver's Travels into Several Remote Nations of the World;* il. by Arthur Rackham. Dutton. Macmillan publishes an attractive edition containing the four voyages, illustrated by C. E. Brock; another good edition is published by Harper, with illustrations by Louis Rhead. First published in 1726 as a satire for adults, Mr. Lemuel Gulliver's account of his shipwreck at sea, his strange adventures among the Lilliputians, and his visit to the giants of Brobdingnag, has been enjoyed by boys and girls as an enchanting fairy tale for more than a century. Ages 10–13.

Thackeray, William Makepeace. *Vanity Fair; a Novel without a Hero.* Dodd. (International Classics.) First published in 1848. This great Victorian novel has many characters, with the unprincipled but fascinating Becky Sharp as central figure. The setting is largely England, with some vivid scenes, including the Battle of Waterloo, on the Continent. Ages 14–15.

CHAPTER XLV

Novels of Today and Yesterday

Coatsworth, Elizabeth. *Here I Stay;* with decorations by Edwin Earle. Coward-McCann, 1938. A pioneer story of a courageous young woman who chose to stay on a Maine farm when her neighbors migrated to Ohio. Ages 12–15.

Farnol, Jeffery. *The Broad Highway;* il. by C. E. Brock. Little, 1911. Romantic story of a disinherited young Englishman who took to the road with ten shillings in his pocket and after many adventures won both fortune and a lady. Ages 12–15.

Field, Rachel. *All This and Heaven Too.* Macmillan, 1938. The story of the French governess who, in 1847, became involved in a famous murder trial; and after she was acquitted came to live in America, where she married an American and presided over a salon in Gramercy Square. Ages 12–15.

Goudge, Elizabeth. *A City of Bells.* Coward-McCann, 1936. A story centering around a bookshop in a quiet cathedral town in England. *Island Magic,* by the same author (Coward-McCann, 1936), tells of an interesting family of young people whose home was in the Channel Islands. Ages 12–15.

Hilton, James. *Lost Horizon.* Morrow, 1933. Four people taking an airplane journey are spirited away to a secret lamasery. An imaginative mystery made believable by the author's skillful handling of his idea. Ages 12–15.

Hope, Anthony. *The Prisoner of Zenda;* il. by Charles Dana Gibson. Holt. First published in 1894. Extraordinary adventures of a young Englishman in an imaginary kingdom in the Austrian Tirol. Ages 12–15.

Hudson, W. H. *Green Mansions; a Romance of the Tropical Forest.* Knopf, 1916. First published in 1904. Based on the naturalist-author's own travels in South America, this story is actual and fantastic at the same time. Ages 12–15.

LaFarge, Oliver. *Laughing Boy*. Houghton, 1929. A present-day novel of the Navajo country, telling of Laughing Boy and Slim Girl, whom he loves. Ages 12–15.

Lane, Rose Wilder. *Let the Hurricane Roar*. Longmans, 1933. A vivid story of early days in Dakota. Ages 12–15.

Orczy, Emmuska. *The Scarlet Pimpernel*. Grosset, 1935. The Scarlet Pimpernel is the leader of a band of Englishmen who, during the French Revolution, helped many aristocrats to escape the guillotine. Ages 12–15.

Rawlings, Marjorie Kinnan. *The Yearling;* decorations by Edward Shenton. Scribner, 1938. This story of young Jody Baxter and his pet fawn gives a very real picture of life on an isolated Florida farm. Ages 11–15.

Tarkington, Booth. *Seventeen: A Tale of Youth and Summer Time and the Baxter Family, Especially William;* il. by Edward Tunis. Harper. First published in 1916. Though full of humor and gentle sarcasm, this story of "Willie" Baxter and his friends shows an understanding sympathy for the problems and absurdities of youth. Ages 12–15.

Wilder, Thornton. *The Bridge of San Luis Rey*. Grosset, 1937. Two hundred years ago an osier bridge made by the Incas collapsed, and five Peruvian travelers were drowned. This story is a retelling and interweaving of inquiries made into the secret lives of the five victims by the Franciscan Brother Juniper. Ages 12–15.

CHAPTER XLVI

Tall Tales

Benét, Stephen Vincent. *The Devil and Daniel Webster;* il. by Harold Denison. Farrar, 1937. A New England legend delightfully and humorously told. Ages 11–15.

Bontemps, Arna and Conroy, Jack. *The Fast Sooner Hound;* il. by Virginia Lee Burton. Houghton, 1942. A "tall tale" from the early days of the railroad, when the hound "Sooner" (so named because he would "Sooner run than eat") raced the fastest train on the road. Fine drawings full of humor and action. Ages 8–12.

Carmer, Carl. *The Hurricane's Children; Tales from Your Neck o' the Woods;* il. by Elizabeth Black Carmer. Farrar, 1937. Twenty humorous American folk tales, including tales of Paul Bunyan, Ichabod Paddock, Kemp Morgan, and Febold Feboldsen. Ages 12–15.

Malcolmson, Anne. *Yankee Doodle's Cousins;* il. by Robert McCloskey. Houghton, 1941. Tales of Paul Bunyan, Mike Fink, Pecos Bill, John Henry, Tony Beaver, and other legendary figures of America. Ages 10–14.

Raspé, Rudolph Erich. *The Adventures of Baron Munchausen;* 160 il. by Gustave Doré. Pantheon Books, Inc., 1944. Wildly improbable and extravagant tales, told with immense seriousness and such careful detail that they almost convince, in spite of the preposterous absurdity of the situations. Doré's amusing and fantastic illustrations helped to make the Baron's adventures famous. First translated into English and published in England in 1785. Ages 10–13.

Rounds, Glen. *Ol' Paul, the Mighty Logger, Being a True Account of the Seemingly Incredible Exploits and Inventions of the Great Paul Bunyan;* profusely il. by drawings made at the scene by the author. Holiday House, 1936. Genuine American folk tales re-told and illustrated with gusto. Other good versions of Paul Bun-yan tales are *Paul Bunyan,* il. by Rockwell Kent, written by Esther Shephard (Harcourt, 1941); and *Paul Bunyan and His Great Blue Ox,* by Wallace Wadsworth (Doubleday, 1941). Ages 9–15.

CHAPTER XLVII

Careers and Occupations

Baarslag, Karl. *SOS to the Rescue;* with a preface by Felix Riesenberg. Oxford, 1935. This tells of the dramatic part played by ships' radiomen when catastrophes occur at sea. Ages 12–15.

Binger, Walter David. *What Engineers Do;* rev. ed. Norton, 1938. The story of civil engineering from the earliest times to the present. Ages 11–13.

Eadie, Thomas. *I Like Diving, a Professional's Story.* Houghton, 1929. An account of the business of a diver, including the raising of the S-4 and S-51. Ages 12–15.

Ellsberg, Edward. *On the Bottom.* Dodd, 1929. The salvage of the submarine S-51, rammed and sunk in 132 feet of water off Block Island. Ages 12–15.

Floherty, John J. *Inside the F.B.I.;* with a foreword by J. Edgar Hoover; il. from photographs. Lippincott, 1943. Tells of the work of the F.B.I. in peace and war, how its men are trained, and its scientific methods of crime detection. Ages 10–15.

Floherty, John J. *Men without Fear.* Lippincott, 1940. This tells of the work and the dangers faced by test pilots, lightship crews, men handling explosives, linesmen, sandhogs, divers, miners, oil-well drillers, newsreel cameramen, and harbor patrolmen. Ages 11–14.

Floherty, John J. *On the Air, the Story of Radio;* foreword by David Sarnoff; il. by the author. Doubleday, 1937. Interesting account, with many pictures, of the way broadcasting stations function. Ages 11–15.

Floherty, John J. *Sons of the Hurricane;* il. by fifty-five action photographs taken by the author. Lippincott, 1938. This describes heroic work of the U.S. Coast Guardsmen. Ages 12–15.

Hewes, Agnes Danforth. *Jackhammer; Drill Runners of the Mountain Highways.* Knopf, 1942. A story of road building in the Western mountains, full of adventure and danger as experienced by the young hero of the tale, who wanted to become an engineer. *The Iron Doctor* (Houghton, 1940), by the same author, is a story of deep-water diving. Ages 11–14.

Klinefelter, Lee Miller. *Medical Occupations Available to Boys When They Grow Up;* il. with photographs. Dutton, 1937. A boy who visits physicians, specialists, technicians, etc., learns, through informal questions and answers, how each man feels about his field of work, how much he earns from it, and the necessary qualifications for each branch of medicine. The author's *Medical Occupations Available to Girls; Women in White,* il. with photographs (Dutton, 1939), is a corresponding book for girls. Ages 12–15.

Lent, Henry Bolles. *Clear Track Ahead!;* il. by Earle Winslow. Macmillan, 1932. This tells how trains are run. Ages 9–11.

Lent, Henry Bolles. *Diggers and Builders.* Macmillan, 1931. Simple explanations of the work done by the steam-shovel man, the cement mixer, derrick man, steel worker, road builder, and truck driver. Ages 8–11.

Meader, Stephen W. *Lumberjack;* il. by H. C. Pitz. Harcourt, 1934. A lively, interesting story with a New Hampshire lumber camp as a background. Ages 11–14.

Zim, Herbert S. *Submarines: The Story of the Undersea Boats;* il. with drawings by James MacDonald and with photographs. Harcourt, 1942. The author presents the history and theory of the submarine, the matter of navigation, use of the periscope, the torpedo, and other weapons. Ages 12–15.

CHAPTER XLVIII

Flying

Adams, Jean and Kimball, Margaret and Eaton, Jeanette. *Heroines of the Sky*. Doubleday, 1942. Tells of the many licensed women pilots in this country, what they have done and are doing. Ages 12–15.

Anderson, Lonzo. *Bag of Smoke; the Story of the First Balloon;* pictures by Adrienne Adams. Viking, 1942. Well-told story of those pioneers in aviation, the Montgolfier brothers who, in 1783, invented the first balloon. Ages 10–13.

Ayling, Keith. *How Every Boy Can Prepare for Aviation Service;* il. by Edward Branford. Garden City Pub. Co., 1942. A former R.A.F. pilot tells how to get ready for a post as pilot, gunner, bombardier, or mechanic. Ages 12–15.

Black, Archibald. *The Story of Flying*. McGraw, 1940. The story of the development of the art of flying, from the legend of Daedalus to the stratosphere liner. Ages 10–15.

Booth, Harold H. *Book of Modern Airplanes;* foreword by Colonel Roscoe Turner. Garden City Pub. Co., 1942. A collection of paintings of the world's latest fighting aircraft. Ages 10–15.

Chapin, Mary K. *Why Man Can Fly;* il. by Alice M. Heun. Reynal, 1943. A brief survey of the history and mechanics of the airplane, weather factors, and the aviator's qualifications. Ages 12–15.

Conger, Elizabeth Mallett. *American Warplanes;* il. and indexed. Holt, 1943. This describes American fighters, bombers, scouting, and training and other types of planes, with chapters on carriers, gliders, and paratroops. Ages 9–11.

De Seversky, Alexander P. *Victory through Air Power*. Simon, 1942. Written for adults, this book also interests boys because of its analysis of the recent war and the defense problems of the United States. Ages 12–15.

Floherty, John J. *Aviation from Shop to Sky*. Lippincott, 1941. Ages 12–15.

Floherty, John J. *'Board the Airliner, a Camera Trip with the Transport Planes*. Doubleday, 1934. Ages 9–11.

Fraser, Chelsea. *Famous American Flyers;* with maps by the author. Crowell, 1941. Ages 11–15.

Gann, Ernest K. *Sky Roads*. Crowell, 1940. The story of the development of commercial aviation, told with enthusiasm. Ages 11–15.

Johnston, Samuel Paul. *Horizons Unlimited*. Duell, 1941. A graphic history of aviation. Ages 10–15.

Keliher, Alice Virginia, ed. *Air Workers Today,* by the Picture Fact Associates; il. Harper, 1942. (Picture Fact Bks., Group 1.) Ages 10–15.

Kinert, R. C. *America's Fighting Planes in Action*. Macmillan, 1943. Fine drawings. Ages 9–15.

Langewiesche-Brandt, Wolfgang Ernst. *I'll Take the High Road*. Harcourt, 1939. The experiences of an amateur flyer. Ages 12–15.

Law, Major Bernard A. *Fighting Planes of the World;* with an introd. by Nathaniel F. Silsbee; il. by Barry Bart; new rev. ed. Random House, 1942. Descriptions of the modern fighting planes, illustrated with color photographs. Ages 8–15.

Lent, Henry B. *Air Patrol: Jim Brewster Flies for the U.S. Coast Guard;* with official U.S. Coast Guard photographs. Macmillan, 1942. The material for this story was gathered at the Brooklyn air station, Floyd Bennett Field. Ages 10–15.

Lindbergh, Anne Morrow. *North to the Orient;* with maps by C. A. Lindbergh. Harcourt, 1935. An account of actual experience, characterized by humor and keen perceptiveness. Ages 11–15.

Lloyd, T. L. *Sky Highways; Geography from the Air*. Houghton, 1945. What one does and what one sees on a flight in the sky highways. Ages 12–15.

Meyer, Dickey. *Planes in Action. How Planes Get There;* drawings by Da Costa; prepared by Aviation Research Associates. Harper, 1945. 2 vols. Clear explanation of the underlying principles of navigation and performance of planes. Ages 9–12.

Neville, Leslie E., ed. *Aviation Dictionary for Boys and Girls;* il. by Gregorio Prestopino. Whittlesey House, 1944. A basic volume for junior aviation libraries. Ages 10–15.

Ott, Lester. *Aircraft Spotter.* Harcourt, 1943. Ages 9–15.

Rifkin, Lillian and Cooke, David C. *When I Grow Up I'll Be a Flyer;* by Lillian Rifkin, with technical assistance from David C. Cooke; il. with photographs. Lothrop, 1942. Information for younger children on the requirements for and the training of army, navy, and civilian pilots. Written in non-technical language. Ages 8–10.

Saint Exupéry, Antoine de. *Wind, Sand and Stars;* trans. from the French by Lewis Galantière; decorations by John O'H. Cosgrave, II. Reynal, 1940. A French aviator writes magnificently of his experiences as airline pilot during the years between 1926 and 1936. Ages 14–15.

Steinbeck, John. *Bombs Away.* Viking, 1942. The story of a bomber team written for the U.S. Army Air Forces. The author describes the intensive training of the individual members of a bomber crew. Ages 12–15.

Winston, Lt. Robert A., U.S.N. *Aircraft Carrier;* il. with official U.S. Navy photographs. Harper, 1942. The development of the aircraft carrier, how it was employed in the early stages of the war, the kind of men who man these ships. Ages 12–15.

Winston, Lt. Robert A., U.S.N. *Dive Bomber;* il. by Walter I. Dothard. Holiday House, 1940. An account of the training and life of the aviators of the U.S. Navy. Ages 12–15.

Young America's Aviation Annual; ed. by Frederick P. Graham and Reginald M. Cleveland; foreword by Gill Robb Wilson; il. with photographs. McBride, 1942. Ages 11–14.

Zim, Herbert S. *Air Navigation;* il. with drawings by James MacDonald and with photographs. Harcourt, 1943. Dead reckoning, radio and celestial navigation are explained. Fifty drawings, diagrams and maps, forty photographs, and an Official Civil Aeronautics Administration navigation chart of the Seattle section of the United States add to the value of the book. Ages 12–15.

Zim, Herbert S. *Parachutes;* il. with drawings by James MacDonald and with photographs. Harcourt, 1942. The history of parachuting. Ages 12–15.

CHAPTER XLIX

Building Model Airplanes

Air Youth of America. *Building and Flying Model Airplanes.* Appleton-Century, 1941. Ages 10–15.

Gilmore, Horace Herman. *Model Planes for Beginners.* Harper, 1942. Ages 9–11.

Hamilton, Edwin Timothy. *Complete Model Aircraft Manual;* plans by the author and Frank Monaghan; new and rev. ed. Dodd, 1938. Ages 10–14.

CHAPTER L

Army and Navy

Brown, Paul. *Insignia of the Services*. Scribner, 1941. Pictures the insignia worn on caps, sleeves, and shoulders of members of the army, navy, marine corps, and air force, including that worn by women. Ages 9–15.

Downey, Fairfax. *Jezebel the Jeep;* il. by Paul Brown. Dodd, 1944. Tells of Private Johnny of the artillery and his devotion to his never-failing jeep. Ages 9–12.

Peet, Creighton. *Defending America;* il. by Fritz Kredel. Harper, 1941. This describes the organization, equipment, supplies, and daily life of each branch of the United States war service on land, sea, or in the air. Many illustrations. Ages 9–13.

CHAPTER LI

The Wonders of Daily Life

WE WHO live in the world of today are surrounded by wonders which we take as a matter of course. Here are books to remind us how much scientific knowledge, technical skill, and efficient organization contribute to the comfort and security of our lives.

Bendick, Jeanne. *Electronics for Boys and Girls;* il. by the author. Whittlesey House, 1944. The development of the science of electronics described clearly and in a way to arouse the reader's interest. Definitions of terms and clever diagrams. Ages 11–13.

Benz, Francis E. *Talking Round the Earth; the Story of the Telephone;* il. with photographs. Dodd, 1942. How man invented and perfected the telephone. Ages 10–14.

Britton, Katharine. *What Makes It Tick?;* il. by Jeanne Bendick. Houghton, 1943. What makes a clock go? Why does electricity light up a room when a switch is turned? How does sound come over the radio? These are a few of the questions which this book answers in simple, satisfying fashion. Many excellent drawings. Ages 7–12.

Eaton, Jeanette. *Behind the Show Window.* Harcourt, 1935. About half the book is devoted to the food industries, several chapters to the textile industries, and one each to electrical goods and automobiles. The book is based on two years of research, and the author has skillfully introduced historical sketches of such commodities as coffee, silk, electricity. Ages 12–15.

Harrison, George Russell. *How Things Work; Science for Young Americans;* il. by James MacDonald. Morrow, 1941. Explanations of modern scientific discoveries and inventions. Ages 10–14.

Henry, Robert S. *Trains*. Bobbs, 1938. A history of railroading in the United States, emphasizing the development of equipment. Ages 10–13.

· Hoadley, Ray. *How They Make a Motion Picture;* photographs by Roman Freulich. Crowell, 1939. The history of the movie industry, scenery and sets, costumes, make-up, photography and lighting, sound, casting, the animated cartoon, newsreel, and other topics. Many excellent photographs. *Let's Go to the Movies,* by W. C. and H. S. Pryor (Harcourt, 1939), suggests standards for critical judgment and comparison of the movies themselves. Ages 12–15.

Hylander, Clarence J. and Harding, Robert. *Introduction to Television*. Macmillan, 1943. What television is, what has been accomplished, what the future may bring. Ages 12–15.

Jackson, Ann. *The Wonders of Oil;* in collaboration with Delmar E. Jackson; il. from official photographs and charts. Dodd, 1940. Simply, and partly in story form, the authors tell what oil is, where it is found, how it was discovered, how it is produced and used. Excellent photographs. Ages 10–13.

Langdon-Davies, John. *Radio: The Story of the Capture and Use of Radio Waves;* il. by Betty Barr. Dodd, 1935. An explanation of the principles of radio, and the history of each step that led to its development. Ages 12–15.

Le May, Geraldine. *The Story of a Dam*. Longmans, 1940. (America at Work.) Clear, simple, readable account of the building of the Norris Dam and the work of the TVA in flood control, reforestation, and the education of the farmer in scientific methods of agriculture. Ages 10–15.

Meader, Stephen W. *The Long Trains Roll;* il. by Edward Shenton. Harcourt, 1944. Tells how enemy sabotage was foiled and gives a fine picture of railroading in this country. Ages 10–14.

Metcalfe, June M. *Copper: The Red Metal*. Viking, 1944. The story of copper, beginning with ancient Egypt and primitive man: how and where it is found, how it is mined and processed. Written with accuracy, liveliness, and charm, and illustrated with magnificent photographs. Ages 10–15.

Morgan, Alfred Powell. *The Pageant of Electricity*. Appleton-Century, 1940. The history of the development of electricity from the discovery of the lodestone to television. Ages 12–15.

Morgan, Alfred Powell. *The Story of Skyscrapers;* il. with photographs and drawings by the author. Farrar, 1934. The complete, detailed account of the building of a skyscraper, written by an engineer. Ages 11–15.

Peet, Creighton. *All about Broadcasting;* photographs by the author. Knopf, 1942. The principles and technique of radio broadcasting. Ages 10–14.

Petersham, Maud and Miska. *The Story Book of Things We Wear: Wool, Cotton, Silk, Rayon*. Winston, 1939. Also published in four separate volumes. Contains legends and information about four important materials. Many illustrations in color. Ages 7–10.

Petersham, Maud and Miska. *The Story Book of Wheels, Ships, Trains, Aircraft*. Winston, 1935. Also published in four separate volumes. Brief, simple text on the history of transportation, with many lovely pictures in color. Ages 7–10.

Reck, Franklin M. *Automobiles from Start to Finish;* rev. ed. Crowell, 1941. The story of motor-driven vehicles. The same author discusses the history and progress of radio in his *Radio from Start to Finish* (Crowell, 1942). In *Power from Start to Finish* (Crowell, 1941), F. M. Reck and A. C. Reck discuss the sources of power—water, wind, coal, and oil—and the machines by means of which man makes use of them. Ages 11–15.

Robins, F. W. *The Story of the Lamp (and the Candle)*; il. Oxford, 1939. Lighting appliances round the world and through the ages. Age 12 on.

Schoenen, Hermann. *The Story Behind Steel*. Knopf, 1944. The story of steel clearly and simply told from mining to production; the Bessemer converter, blast furnace, rolling mill, steel as used in our homes, and the steel that goes into battleships, tanks, and guns. Four pictures in color and a large number of unusual photographs. Ages 10–15.

Shenton, Edward. *Couriers of the Clouds; the Romance of the Air Mail;* with il. by the author; rev. & enl. ed. Macrae, 1937. The history of air mail and the service today, described in interesting, graphic fashion. Ages 10–14.

Silverman, Milton Morris. *Magic in a Bottle.* Macmillan, 1941. The discovery and use of digitalis, quinine, aspirin, sulfanilamide, and other drugs. Ages 12–15.

Tyler, Kingdon S. *Modern Radio;* il. with drawings by James MacDonald and with photographs. Harcourt, 1944. Everything in the field of radio from the construction of the broadcasting studio to the emission of sound waves from the loud speaker, including color television and radar. Age 10 on.

Van Metre, Thurman William. *Trains, Tracks and Travel;* 6th ed. Simmons-Boardman, 1944. A comprehensive survey of American railroads, including such information as the history and development of steam railroads; the railroads and the railroad track; the operation of trains. A sixth edition brings this authoritative book, first published in 1926, up to date. Ages 11–13.

CHAPTER LII

Fun and Nonsense

TRUE nonsense provides a world of its own, a world in which absurdity is the accepted order of the day.

Aspinwall, Alicia. *Short Stories for Short People*. Dutton, 1896. Stories of "quick-running squashes," "never-stop bicycles," and islands where "the Upsidedownians live," told with the serious "make-believe" that characterizes all true nonsense. Ages 7–9.

Atwater, Richard and Florence. *Mr. Popper's Penguins;* il. by Robert Lawson. Little, 1938. A story that delights because of its matter-of-fact handling of the absurd, almost convincing us that it would be quite simple to bring up a family of penguins in a refrigerator and travel about the country exhibiting them. Ages 8–10.

Baker, Margaret. *Tinker Tailor and Other Nonsense Tales;* with il. by Mary Baker. Dodd, 1941. Stories that have the logic of true nonsense and the sturdy wisdom and humor of the folk tale. Illustrated by charming silhouettes that have the same fun and gaiety as the tales. Ages 9–11.

Bangs, J. K. *A Houseboat on the Styx*. Harper, 1895. Describes in humorous fashion a group of famous "shades"—Socrates, Shakespeare, Dr. Johnson, Napoleon, and others—gathered in a houseboat with all modern conveniences, and with Charon as steward. Sprightly conversations and lively discussions provide much entertainment for the reader. Ages 11–15.

Belloc, Hilaire. *Cautionary Verses;* il. album ed.; with the original pictures by B. T. B. and Nicholas Bentley. Knopf, 1941. Contains *Cautionary Tales for Children; New Cautionary Tales; Bad Child's Book of Beasts; More Beasts for Worse Children and Other Nonsense Verses*. All ages.

Bennett, John. *The Pigtail of Ah Lee Ben Loo, with Seventeen Other Laughable Tales and 200 Comical Silhouettes.* Longmans, 1928. Amusing stories, ballads, and verses, illustrated with humorous and spirited silhouettes. Ages 9–12.

Beston, Henry. *The Tree That Ran Away;* il. by Fritz Eichenberg. Macmillan, 1941. "You never know what you can do till you try," said a gnome. "Try." So the tree tried. Its roots came out of the earth and a pair of sturdy brown legs carried it off on its travels, its progress causing considerable consternation among horses, cows, and people. Ages 8–12.

Bright, Robert. *Georgie;* il. by the author. Doubleday, 1944. About an amiable little ghost who has his own troubles finding a house to haunt. No child could dread the dark after he has made the acquaintance of genial Georgie. Ages 7–10.

Bronson, Wilfrid S. *Hooker's Holiday;* il. by the author. Harcourt, 1944. What happened when Prof. Grampus brought Hooker the monkey to the Natural History Museum for observation. The broad humor of drawings and text make no inconsiderable rival to "the comics." Ages 7–10.

Carroll, Lewis. *Hunting of the Snark, an Agony in Eight Fits;* il. by Henry Holiday. Macmillan, 1927. A nonsense narrative poem. It was first published in 1876, and this edition reproduces the original illustrations. Ages 8–12.

Charles, Robert H. *A Roundabout Turn;* drawings by L. Leslie Brooke. Warne, 1930. Leslie Brooke's inimitable drawings and Robert H. Charles's entertaining verses present with charm and humor the "toad who lived on Albury heath," who decided to go out and discover whether the world was really round. Ages 6–12.

Darwin, Bernard and Eleanor. *Tale of Mr. Tootleoo.* Harper, 1926. The authors have created absurd and original nonsense characters that children find delightful. Ages 6–9.

Dickens, Charles. *Magic Fishbone;* il. by F. D. Bedford. Warne. Written in 1868. A genuine and childlike nonsense story with delightful illustrations. Ages 8–10.

Du Bois, William Pène. *The Great Geppy;* written and il. by William Pène Du Bois. Viking, 1940. This tale of the horse who developed a talent for detective work is told with refreshing unexpectedness, and the beautifully made drawings have humor, wit, and imagination. *The Three Policemen,* il. by the author (Viking, 1938), and *The Flying Locomotive* (Viking, 1941), are other books by this author-artist which have the logical absurdity of true nonsense and beautiful and distinguished pictures. Ages 8–11.

Ets, Marie Hall. *Mister Penny.* Viking, 1935. How the farm animals showed gratitude to Mr. Penny for his kindness. A kindly, spontaneous, nonsense story which pleases children. Ages 5–8.

Francis, Joseph G. *Book of Cheerful Cats and Other Animated Animals.* Appleton-Century, 1903. Good-natured fun that has delighted many generations of children. Ages 5–8.

Gilbert, W. S. *Plays and Poems;* preface by Deems Taylor; incl. the complete text of the fourteen Gilbert and Sullivan operas, three other Gilbert plays, and all the *Bab Ballads;* with il. by the author. Random House, 1932. A volume of Gilbert's plays, including the *Bab Ballads,* should be in every child's library. Louis Untermeyer's *The Lost Pirate; Tales from the Gilbert and Sullivan Operas,* il. by Reginald Birch (Harcourt, 1934), consists of seven of the operas retold in story form. With Reginald Birch's gay, humorous drawings, this makes an excellent introduction to the original plays (for ages 9–12). Ages 9–15.

Grahame, Kenneth. *The Reluctant Dragon;* il. by E. H. Shepard. Holiday House, 1938. A tale containing humor, human nature, and gaiety, told in a lovely prose. E. H. Shepard has made the perfect pictures. Ages 4–15.

Hale, Lucretia Peabody. *The Peterkin Papers;* il. by H. M. Brett. Houghton, 1924. (Riverside Bookshelf.) One of the best humorous books ever written for children. It has been continuously popular since the stories of this impractical family first appeared in St. Nicholas in 1874–79. Ages 9–12.

Jerome, Jerome K. *Three Men in a Boat (to Say Nothing of the Dog).* First published in 1889. Scribner, 1943. This casual history of a camping trip never fails to amuse. Ages 10–15.

Lawson, Robert. *Ben and Me; a New and Astonishing Life of Benjamin Franklin, as Written by His Good Mouse, Amos; Lately Discovered, Edited and Illustrated by Robert Lawson.* Little, 1939. This diary kept by the mouse who lived in Franklin's fur cap sheds a gay and humorous light on the well-known episodes of Franklin's life. A nonsense story for all ages. Age 9 on.

Leaf, Munro. *Story of Ferdinand;* il. by Robert Lawson. Viking, 1936. An irresistibly funny account in story and pictures of a bull who wouldn't fight. Age 6 on.

Leaf, Munro. *Wee Gillis;* il. by Robert Lawson. Viking, 1938. An entertaining picture book about a small boy who had difficulty in deciding whether to live in the Highlands or Lowlands of Scotland. Mr. Lawson again shows that, in drawings touched with a robust humor, he can reproduce the atmosphere of an actual country.

Lear, Edward. *The Complete Nonsense Book;* containing all the original pictures and verses, together with new material; ed. by Lady Strachey of Sutton Court; introd. by the Earl of Cromer; 9th ed. Dodd, 1942. A complete collection of the work of the great master of nonsense. All ages.

McKay, Herbert. *Noah and Rabbit, a Nursery Thriller;* with twenty il. by Grace Lodge. Dutton, 1932. A story full of imaginative fun and absurdity that resembles a child's own make-believe. Good to read aloud. Ages 6–10.

Richards, Laura E. *Tirra Lirra; Rhymes Old and New;* il. by Marguerite Davis. Little, 1941. Delightful, spontaneous verses by a true nonsense poet. Ages 9–13.

Seuss, Dr. (T. S. Geisel). *The 500 Hats of Bartholomew Cubbins;* il. by the author. Vanguard, 1938. An original, spontaneous tale about a small boy with a miraculous crop of hats. Ages 6–10.

Thackeray, William Makepeace. *The Rose and the Ring,* by A. A. Titmarsh (pseud.); il. by the author. Macmillan, 1923. Written in 1854. A delightful and witty nonsense story written to amuse a little girl friend of the author. Amusing illustrations. Age 12 on.

Travers, Pamela. *Mary Poppins;* il. by Mary Shepard. Reynal,
1934. The remarkable things that happened after Mary Poppins
blew in with an east wind and became nursemaid to the Banks
family. This is followed by *Mary Poppins Comes Back* (Reynal,
1935), and *Mary Poppins Opens the Door,* il. by Mary Shepard
and Agnes Sims (Reynal, 1943). Ages 8–12.

White, T. H. *The Sword in the Stone.* Putnam, 1939. A thoroughly
delightful combination of absurdity, satire, medieval life, and
grown-up fairy tale. Written for adults, this is enjoyed by readers from eleven on. Good for reading aloud.

CHAPTER LIII

Personal Records

THE lives of real people are often as interesting and exciting as fiction.

Acker, Helen. *Three Boys of Old Russia;* il. by Zhenya Gay. Nelson, 1944. The youth of three great Russians, Leo Tolstoy, Maxim Gorky, and Chaliapin, told with sympathy against the magical background of old Russia—endless fields, birch forests, and cities where moonlight turned the onion-shaped domes into something out of a fairy tale. Ages 12–15.

Adams, Julia Davis. *Stonewall;* il. by Cameron Wright. Dutton, 1931. Gives an authentic picture of a fine and heroic man, emphasizing his part in the Civil War. Ages 12–15.

Baker, Nina Brown. *Juarez, Hero of Mexico;* il. by Marion Greenwood. Vanguard, 1942. This sympathetically told life of the great Mexican liberator helps us to understand Mexican history. *Garibaldi;* il. by Louis Slobodkin. Vanguard, 1944. A well-drawn picture of a stirring historical figure and the dramatic events of his life. *Peter the Great;* il. by Louis Slobodkin. Vanguard, 1943. Vivid portrait, from his early boyhood to his death, of Russia's most famous Tsar. Ages 12–15.

Becker, May Lamberton. *Introducing Charles Dickens;* il. by Oscar Ogg. Dodd, 1940. A life-long lover of Dickens writes of him in a way to inspire other people to make his acquaintance. Ages 12–15.

Benz, Francis E. *Pasteur, Knight of the Laboratory;* il. by James MacDonald. Dodd, 1938. The experiments and discoveries of the great French scientist. Ages 12–15.

Brown, Rose. *American Emperor, Dom Pedro II of Brazil;* il. by C. B. Falls. Viking, 1945. This well-written, readable biography makes a famous name in South American history a very real personality. Ages 12–15.

Buffalo Child Long Lance. *Long Lance.* Farrar, 1928. Tribal life and ceremonies of the Canadian Blackfeet described by Chief Long Lance, who as a boy watched or shared in the experiences described. Ages 12–15.

Curie, Eve. *Madame Curie.* Garden City Pub. Co., 1939. Written for adults, this moving and inspiring book has a strong appeal for older boys and girls. *Radium Treasure and the Curies,* il. by William Sharp (Crowell, 1942), tells, for younger children, of the lives of the two Curies, and of radium today, its nature, properties, and use. Ages 12–15.

Daugherty, James. *Daniel Boone;* with original lithographs in color by the author. Viking, 1939. This brings to life a great-hearted, dauntless pioneer. *Daniel Boone, Wilderness Scout,* by Stewart Edward White, il. by James Daugherty (Garden City Pub. Co., 1933), is another excellent life of Boone. Ages 10–14.

D'Aulaire, Ingri and Edgar Parin. *Leif the Lucky.* Doubleday, 1941. A splendid picture book telling how Leif, son of Eric the Red, sailed as a boy to Greenland and later to the continent of America. The brief text is direct and spirited and the pictures glow with color. Ages 7–10.

Deutsch, Babette. *Walt Whitman; Builder for America;* il. by Rafaello Busoni. Messner, 1941. A thoughtful, sympathetic biography. Nearly half the book consists of a selection of Whitman's poems which young people enjoy. Ages 14–15.

Eaton, Jeanette. *A Daughter of the Seine.* Harper, 1929. The story of Madame Roland, a famous heroine of the French Revolution. *Young Lafayette,* il. by David Hendrickson (Houghton, 1932), by the same author, is a vivid portrait of a romantic figure in American history. Ages 12–14.

Eaton, Jeanette. *Leader by Destiny; George Washington, Man and Patriot;* il. by Jack Manley Rosé. Harcourt, 1938. Well-written, thoughtful biography. *Everybody's Washington,* il. by Mead Schaeffer (Dodd, 1931), will please slightly younger readers. Ages 13–15.

Finta, Alexander and Eaton, Jeanette. *Herdboy of Hungary, the True Story of Mocskos;* il. by Alexander Finta. Harper, 1932. Vivid autobiographical story of a boy's life on a Hungarian cattle ranch, and of a touching friendship between a boy and a horse. Ages 12–14.

Fox, Genevieve. *Wilfred Grenfell;* il. by Mary Reardon. Crowell, 1942. This biography emphasizes the gallantry and wisdom of one of the heroes of the modern world. Ages 12–15.

Graham, Shirley and Lipscomb, George D. *Dr. George Washington Carver, Scientist;* il. by Elton C. Fax. Messner, 1944. An inspiring biography of a great man written by two young people of his own race. Ages 12–15.

Grahame, Mrs. Elspeth. *First Whisper of Wind in the Willows.* Lippincott, 1945. Mrs. Grahame has included charming, intimate reminiscences of her family life, early versions of her husband's work, pictures of Alistair Grahame, for whom *The Wind in the Willows* was originally written, and a story of Pig and Moley not before published. Age 10 on.

Gray, Elizabeth Janet. *Penn.* Viking, 1938. A well-written, very human life of a great American. Ages 12–15.

Gray, Elizabeth Janet. *Young Walter Scott.* Viking, 1935. A biography that reads with the interest of a story. Ages 12–15.

Hall, Anna Gertrude. *Nansen;* il. by Boris Artzybasheff. Viking, 1940. A sympathetic, vivid description of a great man and his achievements. Beautiful pictures give the feeling of the northern country. Ages 12–15.

Harlow, Alvin F. *Joel Chandler Harris (Uncle Remus), Plantation Story-Teller;* il. by W. C. Nims. Messner, 1941. A sympathetic biography which makes the creator of Uncle Remus and Brer Rabbit very real. Ages 12–15.

Hawthorne, Hildegarde. *Happy Autocrat, a Life of Oliver Wen-dell Holmes;* il. by William Merritt Berger. Longmans, 1938. A lively, interesting account of this famous physician and author. Also by Hildegarde Hawthorne: *Concord's Happy Rebel: Henry David Thoreau,* il. by W. M. Berger (Longmans, 1940); *The Poet of Craigie House, the Story of Henry Wadsworth Longfellow,* il. by W. M. Berger (Appleton-Century, 1936); *Romantic Rebel, the Story of Nathaniel Hawthorne,* il. by W. M. Berger (Appleton-Century, 1932); *Youth's Captain, the Story of Ralph Waldo Emerson,* il. by W. M. Berger (Longmans, 1935). Ages 13–15.

Hunt, Mabel Leigh. *Have You Seen Tom Thumb?;* with il. by Fritz Eichenberg. Stokes, 1942. The story of the famous midget, General Tom Thumb, who was discovered by Barnum at the age of five, traveled over the world, met the crowned heads of Europe, and for years was one of the most popular attractions of the circus. Ages 11–14.

Jarden, Mary Louise. *The Young Brontës; Charlotte and Emily, Bramwell and Anne;* with il. in two colors by Helen Sewell. Viking, 1938. Describes the imaginative life of the young Brontës, in their home on the Yorkshire moors. Ages 12–15.

Judson, Clara Ingram. *Boat Builder; the Story of Robert Fulton;* il. by Armstrong Sperry. Scribner, 1940. The story of the *Clermont's* first voyage is told in full. By the same author, *Railway Engineer, the Story of George Stephenson;* il. by E. M. Simon. Scribner, 1941. Ages 9–11.

Keller, Helen. *The Story of My Life.* Doubleday, 1903. Helen Keller, deaf, dumb, and blind from babyhood, learned how to read and speak, went to college, and became one of the outstanding women of the modern world. This autobiography tells of her early years and education. Ages 12–15.

Lawson, Robert. *They Were Strong and Good;* written and il. by Robert Lawson. Viking, 1940. The story of the author's four grandparents and his father and mother, in pictures and brief text, told not because they were great and famous, but because they were strong and good, and typical of most American fore-bears. Ages 9–11.

Lisitzky, Gene. *Thomas Jefferson;* il. by Harrie Wood. Viking, 1933. An excellent biography which gives a vivid picture of America during Jefferson's lifetime. Ages 12–15.

Maurois, André. *Franklin, the Life of an Optimist;* il. by Howard Simon. Didier, 1945. A brief, readable biography with many pictures and written with warm appreciation. Ages 10–15.

Meadowcroft, Mrs. Enid LaMonte. *Benjamin Franklin;* il. by Donald McKay. Crowell, 1941. A biography written with warmth and imagination. The emphasis is laid on Franklin's boyhood and youth. *Abraham Lincoln,* il. by Kurt Wiese (Crowell, 1942), by the same author, tells of Lincoln's life from childhood to his death. Ages 10–12.

Meadowcroft, William Henry. *Boy's Life of Edison;* rev. ed. Harper, 1921. Interesting, intimate account of Edison's life, written by a member of his laboratory staff. Ages 11–13.

Meigs, Cornelia Lynde. *Invincible Louisa.* Little, 1933. Sympathetic biography of Louisa M. Alcott. Many photographs of the Alcott family and the houses in which they lived. Ages 12–15.

Potter, Edna. *Christopher Columbus, the Story of a Great Adventure.* Oxford, 1932. A good first book about Columbus. Based on authentic records and told with simplicity and a feeling for romance. Ages 9–11.

Robinson, Edward. *Lawrence: The Story of His Life;* with an introductory note by A. W. Lawrence; il. with colored frontispiece and thirty-two pages of plates. Oxford, 1935. The author served under Lawrence in his campaign in Arabia. Ages 12–15.

Roos, Ann. *Man of Molokai, the Life of Father Damien;* il. by Raymond Lufkin. Lippincott, 1943. Inspiring account of Father Damien's devotion to the lepers. Ages 12–15.

Rourke, Constance Mayfield. *Audubon;* with twelve colored plates from original Audubon prints; black and white il. by James MacDonald. Harcourt, 1936. The author followed Audubon's trails in Florida, Louisiana, along the Ohio and the Mississippi; and her story of his life and achievements is full of interest. *Boy of the Woods; the Story of John James Audubon,* by Maie Wells and Dorothy Fox, il. by Elinore Blaisdell (Dutton, 1942), is an excellent biography for younger readers. Ages 12–15.

Rourke, Constance Mayfield. *Davy Crockett;* il. by James MacDonald. Harcourt, 1934. Well-told life of a picturesque figure in American frontier history. Ages 12–15.

Sandburg, Carl. *Abe Lincoln Grows Up;* reprinted from *Abraham Lincoln: The Prairie Years;* il. by James Daugherty. Harcourt, 1928. Sandburg writes of Lincoln with sympathy and understanding and a touch of poetry. Ages 12–15.

Scott, Col. Robert L., Jr. *Runway to the Sun;* il. by Ralph Ray. Scribner, 1945. Col. Scott's early life, his unwavering determination to fly, his training and flying experiences at home and abroad up to the beginning of the war. Written in the same informal style, lighted with humor, as his *God Is My Co-Pilot.* Ages 12–15.

Shore, Maxine and Oblinger, M. M. *Hero of Darien: The Story of Vasco Núñez de Balboa.* Longmans, 1941. A vivid, convincing picture of a great man and an appealing personality. Ages 12–15.

Simonds, William A. *Boy with Edison;* with an introd. by Francis Jehl. Sun Dial Press, 1939. The author, when a boy, spent four years in Menlo Park as an assistant to Mr. Edison during the years when the electric light and phonograph were invented. Ages 10–14.

Spencer, Cornelia. *Three Sisters: The Story of the Soong Family of China;* il. by Kurt Wiese. Day, 1939. Told in fiction form, but based on fact. Ages 13–15.

Steffens, Lincoln. *Boy on Horseback;* reprinted from *The Autobiography of Lincoln Steffens;* il. by Sanford Tousey. Harcourt, 1935. This account of the author's boyhood in California in the 1870's reads like a story. Ages 11–15.

Sze, Mai-Mai. *Echo of a Cry;* il. by the author. Harcourt, 1945. The daughter of a Chinese diplomat tells of her girlhood in England, France, and the United States, as well as in China, writing with humor and as a keen observer. Ages 14–15.

Van Loon, Hendrik Willem. *The Life and Times of Simon Bolivar.* Dodd, 1943. Mr. Van Loon not only explains his hero, but gives an over-all view of South American history. Written in lively, informal style and illustrated by spirited line drawings. Ages 12–15.

Van Loon, Hendrik Willem. *Thomas Jefferson: The Serene Citizen from Monticello Who Gave Us an American Way of Thinking and Who Gained World-Wide Renown by His Noble Understanding of That Most Difficult of All Arts, the Art of Living, As He Felt That It Should Be Practised in the Republic of Which He Was One of the Founders;* il. by the author. Dodd, 1943. An informal biography that emphasizes Jefferson's zeal for freedom and presents him against the background of an America in which the spirit of independence was growing. Ages 13–15.

Waldeck, Theodore J. *On Safari;* with il. by Kurt Wiese. Viking, 1940. This partly biographical account of the author's three expeditions to Africa as scientist and photographer is full of interest and excitement and the author's own enthusiasm for wild animals and for exploring. Ages 12–15.

Waugh, Elizabeth. *Simón Bolívar; a Story of Courage;* il. by Flora Nash DeMuth. Macmillan, 1941. The stirring story of a valiant, courageous, and picturesque character. Ages 11–15.

Wiggin, Kate Douglas. *Child's Journey with Dickens.* Houghton, 1912. Delightful account of the author's chance meeting with Dickens on a railway journey when she was a little girl. Age 10 on.

Wood, L. N. *Raymond L. Ditmars; His Exciting Career with Reptiles, Animals and Insects;* il. with photographs. Messner, 1944. Boys and girls find this naturalist's experiences engrossing reading. Ages 12–15.

Wood, L. N. *Walter Reid; Doctor in Uniform;* il. by Douglas Duer. Messner, 1943. Absorbing account of the life of the great bacteriologist who solved the mystery of yellow fever. Ages 12–15.

CHAPTER LIV

Heroes of Today

Ayling, Keith. *Semper Fidelis; the U.S. Marines in Action;* il. with photographs. Houghton, 1943. The training of marines and stories of the corps in action at Guadalcanal, Midway, Wake Island, etc. Ages 12–15.

Banning, Kendall. *Submarine! The Story of Undersea Fighters;* il. by Charles Rosner. Random House, 1942. Invention, history, design of the modern submarine, the submarine in action today. Ages 12–15.

Floherty, John J. *The Courage and the Glory.* Lippincott, 1942. True stories of eight great American heroes of the Second World War. Ages 12–15.

Kennerly, Byron Fees. *The Eagles Roar!;* as told to Graham Berry. Harper, 1942. An American aviator tells of his seven months' experience with the Eagle squadron, the American squadron of the R.A.F. Ages 13–15.

Monks, Noel. *Squadrons Up! A Firsthand Story of the R.A.F.* Mc-Graw, 1941. Stories by a London war correspondent of two Hurricane units of the R.A.F. in France, Dunkirk, and Britain. Describes many air battles against tremendous odds. Ages 13–15.

Trumbull, Robert. *The Raft.* Holt, 1942. The raft is the four-by-eight-foot rubber life-boat in which three naval aviators drifted for thirty-four days in the South Pacific without food, water, or equipment. Ages 12–15.

White, William Lindsay. *They Were Expendable.* Harcourt, 1942. Survivors of Torpedo Boat Squadron 3, assigned to duty in the Philippines, tell in their own words the story of Bataan and Corregidor. Ages 12–15.

CHAPTER LV

Poetry

POETRY makes immortal all that is best and most beautiful.

De la Mare, Walter. *Peacock Pie; a Book of Rhymes;* eighty-one little pictures in color by Jocelyn Crowe; new ed. Holt, 1936. Real
poetry for all ages. Two other volumes of verse by the author
are *Down-a-Down-Derry,* il. by Dorothy Lathrop (Holt, 1922);
Bells and Grass, il. by Dorothy Lathrop (Viking, 1942). Ages
7–15.

Dickinson, Emily. *Poems for Youth;* ed. by A. L. Hampson; il. by
George and Doris Hauman. Little, 1934. A selection of the author's nature poems and others which young people enjoy. Ages
12–15.

Farjeon, Eleanor. *Cherrystones;* il. by Isobel and John Morton-
Sale. Lippincott, 1944. Twenty-four charming fortune-telling
poems that have their inspiration in ancient rhyme charms.
Ages 10–14.

Farjeon, Eleanor. *Joan's Door;* il. by Will Townsend. Stokes, 1933.
Verses about gardens and city streets, birds and flowers, chest-
nuts, fairies, and rainbows. Ages 7–9.

Ferris, Helen, comp. *Love's Enchantment; Story Poems and Ballads;* decorations by Vera Bock. Doubleday, 1944. Twenty-seven
romantic poems enjoyed by girls, that range from "Barbara Allen" to Alfred Noyes's "The Highwayman." Ages 11–15.

Field, Rachel Lyman. *Taxis and Toadstools;* verses and decorations by Rachel Field. Doubleday, 1926. Childlike verses about
things seen in the city and in the country. Ages 7–11.

Fish, Helen Dean. *Four and Twenty Blackbirds; Nursery Rhymes of Yesterday Recalled for Children of Today;* il. by Robert Lawson. Stokes, 1937. Twenty-four old nursery rhymes and ballads with spirited full-page drawings. Ages 5–9.

Fyleman, Rose. *Fairies and Chimneys.* Doubleday, 1920. Verses full of charm and imagination. Ages 9–10.

Housman, A. E. *A Shropshire Lad;* auth. ed. Holt, 1922. A poem sequence, giving a picture of a springtime in the life of a young man in England, much enjoyed by older boys and girls. Ages 12–15.

Kipling, Rudyard. *Rudyard Kipling's Verse;* inclusive ed. 1885–1932. Doubleday, 1934. Kipling wrote many poems that boys and girls enjoy. Ages 10–15.

Lindsay, Vachel. *Johnny Appleseed and Other Poems;* il. by George M. Richards. Macmillan, 1928. Nonsense rhymes and songs for little children, historical poems, and selections from "The Congo" and "The Chinese Nightingale." Ages 9–15.

Macaulay, T. B. *Lays of Ancient Rome.* Houghton. First published in 1842. (Riverside Literature Series.) Stirring narrative poems that boys and girls enjoy. Ages 10–15.

Masefield, John. *Salt-Water Poems and Ballads;* il. by Charles Pears. Macmillan, 1916. Poems about the sea and ships by a poet who knows and loves them. Ages 9–15.

Millay, Edna St. Vincent. *Edna St. Vincent Millay's Poems, Selected for Young People;* il. by J. Paget-Fredericks. Harper, 1929. A collection made up of well-known poems from Miss Millay's other volumes. Ages 12–15.

Milne, A. A. *When We Were Very Young;* il. by E. H. Shepard. Dutton, 1924. Poems for and about little children, full of an imagination which is like the child's own. Ages 5–9.

Robinson, Tom. *In and Out; Verses;* pictures by Marguerite de Angeli. Viking, 1943. Verses and pictures that speak to the little child in a way he perfectly comprehends. Beautiful and distinguished in design and illustrations. Ages 3–6.

Rossetti, Christina G. *Sing Song; a Nursery Rhyme Book;* il. by Marguerite Davis. Macmillan, 1924. (Little Library.) Brief, simple verses with a singing quality. Ages 5–9.

Stevenson, Robert Louis. *Child's Garden of Verses;* il. by J. W. Smith. Scribner, 1905. (Scribner's Illustrated Classics.) Poems full of music and rhythm, by a poet who always kept his ability to live in a child's world. Ages 5–9.

Teasdale, Sara. *Stars To-night; Verses New and Old for Boys and Girls;* il. by Dorothy Lathrop. Macmillan, 1930. The poet herself made this selection from her poems, with young people especially in mind. Ages 11–15.

CHAPTER LVI

Anthologies

Auslander, Joseph and Hill, Frank E. *Winged Horse, the Story of the Poets and Their Poetry;* il. by Paul Honoré. Doubleday, 1927. An account of poetry through the ages, *The Winged Horse Anthology* (Doubleday, 1929), is a companion volume compiled by these two authors. Ages 12–15.

Barnes, Ruth A., comp. *I Hear America Singing; an Anthology of Folk Poetry;* il. by Robert Lawson; with an introd. by Carl Van Doren. Winston, 1937. Folk poems of the westward movement, the gold rush, cowboys, homesteading, lumberjacks, sea chanteys, Negro poems, mountain songs, and habitant verses. Ages 11–16.

Bontemps, Arna, comp. *Golden Slippers; an Anthology of Negro Poetry for Young Readers;* with drawings by Henrietta Bruce Sharon. Harper, 1941. Religious, humorous, lyrical, and narrative poems are included. Many of them are not in dialect. Ages 12–15.

Brewton, John Edmund, comp. *Under the Tent of the Sky;* drawings by Robert Lawson. Macmillan, 1937. "A collection of poems about animals large and small." *Gaily We Parade* (Macmillan, 1940), also compiled by Mr. Brewton, is a collection of poems about people. Ages 8–12.

Daringer, Helen Fern and Eaton, Anne Thaxter, eds. *The Poet's Craft;* il. by Helène Carter. World Book, 1935. A collection of verse meant to teach the appreciation and understanding of poetry, arranged under such headings as "Rhythm"; "Word Music"; "Pictures in Poetry"; "Rhyme, Stanza and Pattern." Includes a wide variety of verse. Ages 10–15.

De la Mare, Walter, comp. *Come Hither;* il. by Alec Buckels; new and rev. ed. Knopf, 1928. "A collection of rhymes and poems for the young of all ages." Ages 10–15.

Harrington, Mildred P., comp. *Ring-a-Round; a Collection of Verse for Boys and Girls;* il. by Corydon Bell. Macmillan, 1930. A collection carefully planned to introduce the child to the magic world of poetry. Ages 2–9.

Thompson, Blanche Jennings, comp. *Silver Pennies, a Collection of Modern Poems for Boys and Girls;* il. by Winifred Bromhall. Macmillan, 1925. (Little Library.) Poems selected with an understanding of children's tastes and interests. *More Silver Pennies,* il. by Pelagie Doane (Macmillan, 1938), contains old favorites and many new ones. *With Harp and Lute,* il. by Kate Seredy (Macmillan, 1935), though planned primarily for Catholic children will appeal to all poetry-loving boys and girls. Ages 8–14.

Untermeyer, Louis, ed. *Rainbow in the Sky;* il. by Reginald Birch. Harcourt, 1935. A wide selection of poetry with delightful drawings full of gaiety and a delightful humor. Ages 8–12.

Untermeyer, Louis, ed. *This Singing World: an Anthology of Modern Poetry for Young People;* il. by F. W. Ivins. Harcourt, 1923. An excellent selection of poems which have a real appeal to boys and girls. *Stars to Steer By,* il. by Dorothy Bayley (Harcourt, 1941), is another excellent collection made by the same compiler. Ages 9–15.

Wiggin, Kate Douglas and Smith, Nora Archibald, eds. *Golden Numbers, Poems for Children and Young People.* Doubleday, 1902. A collection made with understanding of the interests of boys and girls. Ages 9–15.

CHAPTER LVII

Plays That Are Fun to Read

Barrie, Sir James M. *The Plays of J. M. Barrie.* Scribner, 1928. Contains *Peter Pan, A Kiss for Cinderella, What Every Woman Knows, Dear Brutus, The Twelve Pound Look,* and others. Ages 12–15.

Gregory, Lady. *Seven Short Plays.* Putnam, 1909. Contents: *Spreading the News, Hyacinth Halvey, Rising of the Moon, Jackdaw, Workhouse Ward, Traveling Man, Gaol Gate.* Ages 12–15.

Howard, Sidney and De Kruif, Paul. *Yellow Jack;* a history in collaboration with Paul De Kruif; il. by Jo Mielziner. Harcourt, 1933. A dramatization of the story of the fight against yellow fever. Ages 12–15.

Lamb, Charles and Mary. *Tales from Shakespeare;* il. by Maud and Miska Petersham. Macmillan, 1923. (Children's Classics.) These stories of Shakespeare's plays, written many years ago, are still the best introduction to the plays themselves. Ages 9–12.

Noyes, Alfred. *Sherwood; or, Robin Hood and the Three Kings.* Lippincott, 1921. A poetic play centering around Robin Hood. Ages 12–15.

O'Neill, Eugene. *The Emperor Jones.* Appleton, 1925. A thrilling play based on a study of fear. Ages 12–15.

Rostand, Edmond. *Cyrano de Bergerac;* trans. by Brian Hooker. Holt, 1937. A delightful play full of action, humor, swordplay, and romance. Ages 12–15.

Shakespeare, William. *Julius Caesar;* arr. and condensed for Little Theatre production with stage directions, notes, and designs for scenery and costumes by Thomas P. Robinson. Viking, 1942. (The Players' Shakespeare.) Also: *A Midsummer Night's Dream,*

The Taming of the Shrew, As You Like It, Macbeth, The Tempest. Not only very useful to anyone who wants to produce a Shakespeare play, but fun to read. In *Three Children and Shakespeare* (Harper, 1938), Anne Terry White uses the device of a mother reading and discussing the plays with her children to present many fresh and interesting ideas. For readers 10–12.

Sherwood, Robert Emmet. *Abe Lincoln in Illinois.* Scribner, 1939. Episodes in the life of Lincoln from 1830–61 presented in moving fashion. Ages 12–15.

Synge, John M. *Riders to the Sea.* Luce, 1911. A short tragic play of great beauty. Ages 12–15.

Wilder, Thornton. *Our Town; a Play in Three Acts;* actor's ed. Coward, 1939. The everyday living, marrying, and dying of the townsfolk of Grover's Corners, New Hampshire. Ages 14–15.

Yeats, William Butler. *The Land of Heart's Desire.* (In *Atlantic Book of Modern Plays,* ed. by Sterling Andrus Leonard; rev. ed. Little, 1934.) Poetic play based on a fairy legend. Ages 12–15.

CHAPTER LVIII

Plays to Act

Barnes, Emily Ann and Young, Bess M., comps. *Plays, Dramatizations by Sixth-Grade Children;* pub. for Lincoln School, Teachers College, 1932. (Lincoln School Children's Series.) Plays which boys and girls made and acted, using material from the following: "Padraig of the Scriptorium," from L. Lamprey's *Masters of the Guild; The Boy Knight of Reims,* by Eloise Lownsbery; *The Goldsmith of Florence,* by Katharine Gibson; *The Magic Fishbone,* by Charles Dickens; two old English ballads. Photographs of settings and costumes. Ages 11–13.

Coulter, Sally. *Footlight Fun; a Book of Plays for Grades 6–10.* Silver, 1941. Comedy, fantasy, and nonsense. Ages 11–14.

Moses, Montrose J., ed. *Ring Up the Curtain;* il. by J. L. Scott. Little, 1932. A varied collection of twelve plays, suitable for children to act, with considerable range in age. Ages 10–15.

Tobitt, Janet and White, Alice. *One-Act Trips Abroad.* Dutton, 1943. Plays with foreign settings, which have their origin in folklore and history. Ages 9–12.

Willison, George F. ed. *Let's Make a Play; Twelve Plays by Children with a Discussion and Explanation of Dramatic Techniques.* Harper, 1940. The plays include an Eskimo play by the seven- and eight-year-olds, a Christmas play by eight-year-olds; *Fang Tsi Chu,* a Chinese play by eleven-year-olds; *Call to Freedom,* a dramatization of the Underground Railroad by twelve-to-fourteen-year-olds, etc. Ages 7–14.

CHAPTER LIX

What to Do and How to Do It

Bonner, Mary Graham. *Couriers of the Sky*. Knopf, 1944. A useful book for any boy or girl who undertakes to raise pigeons. Ages 10–14.

Collins, Archie Frederick. *Fun with Electricity; a How-to-Make-It Book of Simple and Startling Experiments with Direct, Alternating, and High Frequency Electric Currents*. Appleton-Century, 1936. Ages 12–15.

Collins, Archie Frederick. *Radio Amateur's Handbook;* 8th ed. rev. by E. L. Bragdon. Crowell, 1940. A practical guide to radio construction and repair. Ages 12–15.

Daugherty, Charles Michael. *So Sailors Say;* written and il. by Charles Michael Daugherty. Holt, 1941. A good story combined with practical information about boatbuilding and sailing. Ages 10–14.

Fish, Helen Dean. *The Doll House Book;* il. and diagrams by Hilda Richman. Stokes, 1940. How to build a doll house and furnish it to scale. Suggests a fascinating hobby. Ages 9–15.

Freeman, Mae and Ira. *Fun with Chemistry*. Random House, 1944. Twenty-five interesting and safe experiments which show the basic principles of chemistry and which can be made at home with materials found in the kitchen or the medicine cabinet. Ages 10–14.

Freeman, Mae and Ira. *Fun with Science*. Random House, 1943. Some facts of science presented through simple experiments which can be performed at home. Ages 10–13.

Hawkins, Nancy. *Let's Cook; a Cookbook for Beginners of All Ages;* with decorations by Arthur Hawkins, Jr. Knopf, 1942. A guide to what the beginner needs to know about kitchen equipment, food values, and how to prepare meals. Ages 10–14.

Keelor, Katharine L. *Working with Electricity; a Book of Lights, Bells, Magnets and Messages;* il. by Herbert Plimpton. Macmillan, 1929. Simple, interesting experiments in practical electricity. Ages 9–11.

Leeming, Joseph. *Fun with Magic; How to Make Magic Equipment; How to Perform Many Tricks, Including Some of the Best Tricks of Professional Magicians, and How to Give Successful Magic Shows;* drawings by Jessie Robinson. Stokes, 1943. Includes tricks that are easy to do and which require few properties. Ages 8–12.

Mason, Bernard S. *The Junior Book of Camping and Woodcraft;* drawings by Frederic H. Kock. A. S. Barnes, 1943. Information for the camper on what to wear, what to take, tenting, fire making, cooking, smoke signals, etc. Ages 9–15.

Morgan, Alfred Powell. *Boy Electrician;* il. with new drawings by the author; rev. ed. Lothrop, 1940. A useful book on magnets, cells, telegraph, telephone, radio, etc. Includes experiments which boys can carry out themselves. Ages 11–15.

Morgan, Alfred Powell. *First Radio Book for Boys.* Appleton-Century, 1941. Describes in detail the construction of radio receivers. Ages 11–15.

Morgan, Alfred Powell. *Things a Boy Can Do with Chemistry;* il. by the author. Appleton-Century, 1940. Contains more than 100 experiments. Ages 12–15.

Morgan, Alfred Powell. *Things a Boy Can Do with Electricity;* il. by the author. Scribner, 1938.

Mulholland, John. *Magic in the Making; a First Book of Conjuring;* il. with diagrams and drawings. Scribner, 1925.

Wulff, Lee. *Let's Go Fishing!;* il. by the author. Stokes, 1939. A book on fresh-water fishing which tells about tackle, bait, and kinds of fish. Ages 10–15.

Yates, Raymond F. *A Boy and a Motor;* il. with photographs and drawings by the author. Harper, 1944. Practical information and clear directions for the boy who wants to build simple motors. Ages 10–15.

CHAPTER LX

Marionettes and Puppets

Ficklen, Alexander. *A Handbook of Fist Puppets;* with reproductions from photographs, and numerous line drawings by Julie Brown. Stokes, 1935. Detailed instructions on how to make fist puppets and how to produce a puppet play. Ages 10–14.

Jagendorf, M. *Penny Puppets, Penny Theatre, and Penny Plays;* il. by Fletcher Clark. Bobbs, 1941. Practical directions for making puppets and various types of theaters. Nine brief puppet plays are included. Ages 10–13.

Mills, Mrs. W. H. and Dunn, Mrs. L. M. *Marionettes, Masks, and Shadows;* il. by Corydon Bell. Doubleday, 1927. Practical instructions for mounting and producing puppet shows, masks, and shadow plays, with brief accounts of the historical background for these forms of drama. Ages 12–15.

Rossbach, Charles Edmund. *Making Marionettes.* Harcourt, 1938. Directions for making puppets of both wood and cloth and for building and setting the stage. Ages 10–14.

Warner, Frances Lester. *Ragamuffin Marionettes;* il. by Margaret Freeman. Houghton, 1932. Home-made puppets and how to manage them. Ages 9–11.

CHAPTER LXI

Be at Ease

Boykin, Eleanor. *This Way Please: A Book of Manners;* with il. by Chichi Lasley. Macmillan, 1940. In an informal, pleasant style the author attempts to show young people of high-school age how they should behave at home, in school, in business, and in social situations, and also to suggest why they should adopt these standards. Ages 12–15.

Bro, Marguerite. *Let's Talk about You.* Doubleday, 1945. With humor and imagination, aided by her quick perception and wide acquaintance with young people, the author discusses the problems which normally confront girls in their teens. Much more than a book on manners and etiquette. Ages 12–15.

Clark, Mary E. and Quigley, Margery C. *Etiquette Jr.;* il. by Erick Berry. Doubleday, 1926. In entertaining fashion this covers the entire subject of manners for boys and girls, from table manners and conversation, to school, traveling, and the first job. Ages 10–13.

Giles, Nell. *Susan Be Smooth!; a Handbook of Good Grooming for Girls.* Hale, 1940. Gives good advice on the care of hair and skin, make-up and clothes. Ages 13–15.

CHAPTER LXII

Sports

Allen, Ethan. *Major League Baseball*. Macmillan, 1938. Ages 10–15.

Baldwin, Arthur H. *Junior Skipper's Handbook;* written and il. by Arthur H. Baldwin. Random House, 1940. A guide to sailing for boys and girls. Another good book on sailing is *Learning to Sail* (Macmillan, 1932), by H. A. Calahan. Ages 12–15.

Graham, Frank. *Lou Gehrig, a Quiet Hero*. Putnam, 1942. Ages 10–15.

Haislet, Edwin L. *Boxing*. Barnes, 1940. Ages 12–15.

Henie, Sonja. *Wings on My Feet*. Prentice, 1940. Ages 12–15.

Jackson, Carl H. and Swan, L. A. *Better Badminton*. Barnes, 1939. Ages 12–15.

Jessee, Daniel Edward. *Baseball*. Barnes, 1939. Ages 10–15.

Keith, Harold. *Sports and Games*. Crowell, 1941. Historical accounts of the origin of certain games, as well as tips for players and up-to-date directions, with diagrams. Ages 10–15.

Rice, Grantland and Powel, Harford, eds. *Omnibus of Sport;* il. by Lee Townsend. Harper, 1932. A collection of short stories, news reports, and brief selections from literature dealing with sports. Ages 12–15.

Tunis, John. *The Kid from Tompkinsville;* il. by J. H. Barnum. Harcourt, 1940. A baseball story, followed by *World Series*, il. by J. H. Barnum (Harcourt, 1941). Ages 10–14.

Tunis, John. *Sport for the Fun of It;* il. by Johan Bull. Barnes, 1940. A handbook of information on twenty sports. Ages 10–15.

CHAPTER LXIII

Artists and Their Work

Berry, Ana M. *Art for Children;* 2d ed. Studio, 1934. A well-selected, stimulating collection of beautiful pictures, beautifully reproduced, chosen from the works of great artists of all periods all over the world. Ages 9–15.

Gibson, Katharine. *Goldsmith of Florence; a Book of Great Craftsmen.* Macmillan, 1929. A series of stories about Cellini, Donatello, Della Robbia, Paul Revere, and others. Splendid illustrations. Ages 10–15.

Gibson, Katharine. *Pictures to Grow Up With;* ed. by Bryan Holme. Studio, 1942. More than 120 reproductions of famous paintings and art objects of many lands and ages, arranged under subject. Ages 10–15.

Hillyer, V. M. and Huey, Edward G. *Child's History of Art.* Appleton-Century, 1933. Painting, sculpture, and architecture through the ages. Presented in lively, interesting fashion. Ages 11–14.

Lansing, Elisabeth Hubbard. *Leonardo, Master of the Renaissance;* with il. by William Sharp and an introd. by Hendrik Willem Van Loon. Crowell, 1942. A book which makes an outstanding figure and extraordinary personality, and the fifteenth century in which he lived, very much alive. Ages 12–15.

Naramore, Elisabeth. *William and His Friends; a Group of Notable Creatures in the Metropolitan Museum of Art.* Viking, 1936. This little volume contains twenty-six photographs, ranging from jerboa mice made by an Egyptian potter in 2000 B.C. to one of Herbert Haseltine's modern mares. A valuable bit of training in art appreciation. ("William" is a blue faïence hippopotamus from Egypt.) Ages 8–15.

Wheeler, Opal and Deucher, Sybil. *Giotto Tended the Sheep;* il. by Dorothy Bayley. Dutton, 1938. Appealing little biography, charmingly illustrated, of an early Italian painter. Ages 8–10.

CHAPTER LXIV

Architecture

Lamprey, L. *All the Ways of Building;* il. by Helène Carter. Macmillan, 1933. Traces the history of architecture from the huts of primitive man to modern skyscrapers. Ages 10–13.

Robinson, Ethel Fay and Robinson, T. P. *Houses in America;* more than 150 illustrations by Thomas P. Robinson. Viking, 1936. A history of domestic architecture in this country, many beautiful illustrations of old houses and details of their construction. Ages 12–15.

CHAPTER LXV

Music and Music Makers

Bauer, Marion and Peyser, Ethel R. *How Music Grew;* new rev. ed. with an introd. by W. J. Henderson. Putnam, 1940. Music from prehistoric times to the present day. Ages 12–15.

Bunn, H. F. *Johann Sebastian Bach;* il. by Rafaello Busoni. Random House, 1942. Simple biography telling of the man and the conditions that made him what he was. Ages 10–14.

Coleman, Satis N. *Creative Music in the Home.* Day, 1939. Music stories, how to make instruments, how to play them, and many tunes to play. *The Drum Book* (Day, 1931), by the same author, is a brief history of drums, including those of Africa, India, and the American Indian. Directions for home-made drums and suggestions for playing them. Ages 11–14.

Diller, Angela. *The Story of Lohengrin;* retold and arranged with twenty-one motifs from Wagner's opera and four easy piano transcriptions. Schirmer, 1932. Also, by the same author, *The Story of Siegfried,* il. by Lynd Ward (Smith, 1931). Ages 9–13.

Ewen, David. *Tales from the Vienna Woods: The Story of Johann Strauss;* il. by Edgar Cirlin. Holt, 1944. A well-written, sympathetic life of "the Waltz King," with romantic, enchanting nineteenth-century Vienna as a background for the Strauss family and their music. Ages 12–15.

Goss, Madeleine. *Beethoven, Master Musician.* Doubleday, 1931. The author helps her readers to understand both the vigorous personality of the man and the creative artist's struggle for expression. Her *Deep Flowing Brook,* il. by E. Blaisdell (Holt, 1938), is an interesting portrait of Johann Sebastian Bach against a well-realized background of the eighteenth century. *Unfinished Symphony; the Story of Franz Schubert,* il. by K. M. Schultheiss (Holt, 1941), by the same author, suggests the lovable character of this musician and the genius of the man who compressed the achievement of a lifetime into a few short years. Ages 12–15.

Humphreys, Dena. *On Wings of Song;* il. by Phyllis Coté. Holt, 1944. The story of Mendelssohn, who won early fame and never lost it. His generous nature and absolute integrity set forth against a background of his times and his contemporaries. Age 12 on.

Peter and the Wolf; by Serge Prokofieff; with a foreword by Serge Koussevitzky; designed and il. by Warren Chappell; calligraphy by Hollis Holland. Knopf, 1940. An old Russian folk tale retold for children, with the themes from Prokofieff's opera included. Delightful pictures in color. Ages 8–10.

Stokowski, Olga Samaroff. *The Magic World of Music; a Music Book for the Young of All Ages;* il. by Emil Preetorius. Norton, 1936. Musical information presented in the form of an entertaining fairy tale. The author's *A Musical Manual* (Norton, 1936) is a companion volume. Ages 9–12.

Weber, Henriette. *Prize Song; Stories of Famous Operas;* il. by M. A. Lawson. Oxford, 1935. The stories of fifteen operas told in clear, interesting fashion. The author suggests the musical and dramatic value of each opera, and the main themes from the score are included. Ages 11–15.

Wheeler, Opal and Deucher, Sybil. *Mozart, the Wonder Boy;* il. by Mary Greenwalt; new enl. ed. Dutton, 1941. Pleasantly told story of Mozart's life, with emphasis on his boyhood. Selections from his music are included. Other biographies of musicians by the same authors are *Joseph Haydn, the Merry Little Peasant* (Dutton, 1936); *Edward MacDowell and His Cabin in the Pines* (Dutton, 1940). *Ludwig Beethoven and the Chiming Tower Bells,* il. by Mary Greenwalt (Dutton, 1942); and *Handel at the Court of Kings,* il. by Mary Greenwalt (Dutton, 1943), are by Opal Wheeler. Ages 9–12.

CHAPTER LXVI

Songs

Carmer, Carl. *America Sings; Stories and Songs of Our Country's Growing;* collected and told by Carl Carmer; musical arrangements by Edwin John Stringham; il. in color by Elizabeth Black Carmer. Knopf, 1942. Words and music of twenty-nine American folk songs. For each song, the compiler tells a story about a phase in America's development and illustrates it with a folk tale. Ages 9–14.

Castagnetta, Grace and Van Loon, H. W. *Christmas Carols; Illustrated and Done into Simple Music.* Simon, 1937. Twenty Christmas carols, with brief historical notes and large bright pictures. All ages.

Coleman, Satis N. and Bregman, Adolph. *Songs of American Folks;* il. by Alanson Hewes. Day, 1942. Forty-seven songs collected with enthusiasm and imagination. The compilers have a wide acquaintance with different parts of the country. Will encourage singing in communities, schools, and families. Ages 9–15.

Coleman, Satis N. *Gingerbread Man, and Other Songs of the Children's Story-Book Friends;* il. by Ruth Hambidge. Day, 1931. Eleven popular tales, such as "Johnny Crow," "Little Black Sambo," and "The Three Bears," arranged as songs and set to simple tunes. Ages 5–6.

Crane, Walter. *Pan Pipes; a Book of Old Songs.* Warne, 1900. Old English songs, with many illustrations by Crane. Set to music by Theodore Marzials. Ages 10–15.

Henius, Frank. *Songs and Games of the Americas;* il. by Oscar Fabrés. Scribner, 1943. Games and songs played and sung by the children of South and Central America. The music and the English translation for the songs are included, and there are attractive illustrations in color. Ages 7–12.

Jacobs, Gertrude, comp. *The Chinese-American Song and Game Book;* il. by Chao Chih Chen; music by Virginia and Richard Mather. Barnes, 1944. The rhymes are given in both Chinese and English and have been fitted into Chinese-like melodies so simple that quite young children enjoy learning and singing them. Gay and charming pictures made by a young Chinese girl. Ages 7–10.

Noble, T. Tertius, comp. *Round of Carols;* il. by Helen Sewell. Oxford, 1935. Thirty-five carols of all seasons and all ages in a book that is beautiful in design, typography, and illustration. All ages.

Potter, Edna, comp. *This Way and That; a Book of Singing Games.* Oxford, 1930. An attractive book that will familiarize children with the traditional singing games and will also serve as a picture book; for the artist-compiler has provided a childlike, imaginative illustration in the spirit of every game included. Ages 5–8.

Siegmeister, Elie. *Work and Sing: A Collection of the Songs That Have Built America.* William R. Scott, 1944. A collection of America's work songs of yesterday and today. Songs of the sea, of the West, of railroads, and river boats, with commentary and annotations. Age 9 on.

Trent-Johns, Altona. *Play Songs of the Deep South;* il. by James A. Porter. The Associated Publishers, Inc., 1944. Twelve singing games as played by Negro children in the South, and a Negro lullaby, arranged simply enough to be played and sung by young pianists and used by teachers of folk dancing. Age 9 on.

Van Loon, Hendrik Willem, ed. *The Songs We Sing; a Small Collection of the Songs That Have Been Sung for a Great Many Years by the Children of All Lands;* pictures and text by the editor; music arr. by Grace Castagnetta. Simon, 1936. A picture-song book containing twenty-five songs. Ages 5–8.

Wheeler, Opal. *Sing for America;* pictures by Gustaf Tenggren. Dutton, 1944. Twenty-four American songs—spirituals, cowboy ballads, and patriotic songs—with simple musical arrangements. All ages.

CHAPTER LXVII

Christmas

Bernhard, Josephine. *Lullaby; Why the Pussy-Cat Washes Himself So Often; a Folktale Adapted from the Polish;* pictures by Irene Lorentowicz. Roy, 1944. A legend of the little dusty cat who had to wash himself from chin to tail before he could sing the lullaby which alone could put the Christ Child to sleep. Age 6 on.

Crothers, Samuel McChord. *Miss Muffet's Christmas Party.* Houghton, 1929. This tells how the spider and Miss Muffet planned a literary party and invited the book people. All the perennial story-book favorites, from Cinderella and Alice to Mowgli and Uncle Remus, are brought together with a delicious humor and imaginative understanding. Excellent for reading aloud. All ages.

Dalgliesh, Alice. *Christmas, a Book of Stories Old and New;* il. by Hildegarde Woodward. Scribner, 1934. Many outstanding authors are represented in this varied collection. Ages 9–12.

Duvoisin, Roger. *The Christmas Whale;* il. by the author. Knopf, 1945. An amusing story of the way in which a friendly whale helped Santa Claus out of an awkward situation when all of his reindeer came down with flu eight days before Christmas. Ages 4–10.

Eaton, Anne Thaxter, comp. *The Animals' Christmas; Poems, Carols and Stories;* chosen by Anne Thaxter Eaton; decorated by Angelo Valenti. Viking, 1944. Poems and stories which have to do with animals at Christmas time. Age 7 on.

Field, Rachel. *All Through the Night.* Macmillan, 1940. This tiny book retells the story of the first Christmas Eve as it seemed to the animals in the stable at Bethlehem. Ages 9–15.

Molnár, Ferenc. *The Blue-Eyed Lady;* il. in color by Helen Sewell. Viking, 1942. The tale of a little miracle brought to pass at Christmas time by love and faith. Illustrated in lovely color. Ages 8–10.

Monsell, Helen A. *Paddy's Christmas;* il. by Kurt Wiese. Knopf, 1942. A gay, friendly little tale of a bear cub who found out why "Christmas is pretty, lots of fun and makes you feel good from the inside out." Amusing illustrations and the repetition little children enjoy. Ages 5–7.

Moore, Anne Carroll. *Nicholas, a Manhattan Christmas Story;* il. by Jay Van Everen. Putnam, 1924. A story that catches the flavor of New York and the holiday season. Ages 9–12.

Moore, Clement C. *'Twas the Night before Christmas; a Visit from St. Nicholas;* with pictures by Jessie Willcox Smith. Houghton, 1912. One of the best-known and best-loved of all Christmas poems. The same, with title *The Night Before Christmas,* is published by Lippincott with distinguished illustrations by Arthur Rackham. Ages 9–12.

Potter, Beatrix. *Tailor of Gloucester.* Warne, 1903. A reader of any age can enjoy this lovely Christmas story which mingles snowy streets, old houses, midnight chimes, folk tale and legend, and a kindly spirit. Ages 6–8.

Potter, Beatrix. *Wag-by-Wall;* decorations by J. J. Lankes. The Horn Book, 1944. A warm-hearted, homely Christmas story of the Westmorland country the author knew and loved so well. Age 7 on.

Rey, H. A. *We Three Kings, and Other Christmas Carols;* il. by H. S. Rey. Harper, 1944. Ten of the most familiar carols, with words and music for piano. For each carol there is a gay and reverent picture in color and a picture-note arrangement of the melody. A book to encourage family singing and add to the gaiety of Christmas. Age 6 on.

Sawyer, Ruth. *The Christmas Anna Angel;* il. by Kate Seredy. Viking, 1944. Gay and beautiful Hungarian pictures help to tell this imaginative, heart-warming story of a little girl's Christmas in a hard year of the First World War. Age 7 on.

Sawyer, Ruth. *The Long Christmas;* il. by Valenti Angelo. Viking, 1941. Thirteen Christmas stories taken from ancient legends and interspersed with carols and Christmas rhymes that deepen for readers of all ages the significance of the Christmas season.

The Shining Tree, and Other Christmas Stories. Knopf, 1940. Stories planned for reading rather than telling. A collection for the whole family to enjoy. Elsie Singmaster's *Stories to Read at Christmas* (Houghton, 1940) contains seventeen short stories, all with a fine human quality. Ages 10–15.

Smith, Elva Sophronia and Hazeltine, Alice Isabel. *The Christmas Book of Legends and Stories;* il. by Roger Duvoisin. Lothrop, 1944. New and enlarged edition of this well-chosen collection of poems, legends, and stories of the Christ-child or of the Christmas spirit. Age 9 on.

Thoburn, Jean, comp. and il. *Away in a Manger; Christmas Verse,* selected and decorated by Jean Thoburn. Oxford, 1942. An anthology of Christmas poetry selected with rare taste and a reverent feeling for the meaning of Christmas. Old favorites are included, but many of the poems and carols will be new to most readers. All ages.

Tudor, Tasha. *Snow before Christmas.* Oxford, 1941. A simple little story and delightful pictures in color show us an old-fashioned country Christmas as seen through a child's eyes. Ages 6–8.

Van Stockum, Hilda. *Kersti and Saint Nicholas;* written and il. by Hilda van Stockum. Viking, 1940. About a small Dutch girl so naughty that she even persuaded St. Nicholas to give his presents to the bad children instead of the good ones. Full of fun and childlike mischief and illustrated with delightful colored pictures. Ages 8–10.

CHAPTER LXVIII

A Few Present-Day Picture Books and Illustrated Editions

Aesop's Fables; ed. and il. with wood engravings by Boris Artzybasheff. Viking, 1933. All ages.

Aldin, Cecil. *Dog Day.* Dutton, 1907. No one has drawn more delightful dogs than this English illustrator. All ages.

Ardizzone, Edward. *Little Tim and the Brave Sea Captain.* Oxford, 1936. Ages 5–7.

Bemelmans, Ludwig. *Golden Basket;* il. by the author. Viking, 1936. Ages 9–12.

Beskov, Elsa. *Aunt Green, Aunt Brown, and Aunt Lavender;* il. by the author; trans. from the Swedish by Siri Andrews. Harper, 1928. Ages 6–9.

Bible. *A First Bible;* sel. and arr. by J. W. Maury; il. by Helen Sewell. Oxford, 1934. Ages 9–15.

Bishop, Claire Huchet and Wiese, Kurt. *The Five Chinese Brothers.* Coward-McCann, 1938. Kurt Wiese's fine drawings make this retelling of a folk tale into an amusing picture book. Ages 6–9.

Brooke, L. Leslie. *Ring o' Roses; a Nursery Rhyme Picture Book;* with numerous drawings in color and black and white by Leslie Brooke. Ages 4–8.

Bunyan, John. *Pilgrim's Progress;* drawings by Robert Lawson; retold by Mary Godolphin. Stokes, 1939. First published in 1884. Ages 9–12.

Buff, Mary and Conrad. *Kobi: A Boy of Switzerland;* lithographs by Conrad Buff. Viking, 1936. Ages 9–11.

Burton, Virginia Lee. *The Little House;* story and pictures by V. L. Burton. Houghton, 1943. Ages 6–10.

Daugherty, James. *Andy and the Lion.* Viking, 1938. Ages 6–8.

D'Aulaire, Ingri and Edgar Parin. *Leif the Lucky.* Doubleday, 1941. Ages 7–11.

Du Bois, William Pène. *The Three Policemen; or, Young Botsford of Farbe Island;* written and illustrated by W. P. du Bois. Viking, 1938. Ages 9–11.

Gág, Wanda. *Millions of Cats.* Coward-McCann, 1928. Ages 6–8.

Horn, Madeline Darrough. *Farm on the Hill;* il. by Grant Wood. Scribner, 1936. Ages 7–10.

Jones, Wilfred. *How the Derrick Works.* Macmillan, 1930. Ages 8–12.

Lathrop, Dorothy P. *The Fairy Circus.* Macmillan, 1931. Ages 9–11.

McCloskey, Robert. *Make Way for Ducklings.* Viking, 1941. Ages 5–8.

Newberry, Clare Turlay. *Marshmallow;* story and pictures by C. T. Newberry. Harper, 1942. Ages 5–8.

Petersham, Maud and Miska. *The Christ Child, As Told by Matthew and Luke;* made by Maud and Miska Petersham. Doubleday, 1931. Ages 5–12.

Potter, Beatrix. *Tailor of Gloucester.* Warne, 1903. Ages 6–10.

Seredy, Kate. *The White Stag;* written and il. by the author. Viking, 1935. Ages 10–15.

Smith, E. Boyd. *Prehistoric Animals.* Houghton, 1943. Ages 6–10.

CHAPTER LXIX

The History of Books and Books of Long Ago

Dalgliesh, Alice. *A Book for Jennifer; a Story of London Children in the Eighteenth Century and of Mr. Newbery's Juvenile Library; Embellished with Ten Elegant Drawings by Katherine Milhous, to Which Are Added Eleven Cuts from Old Books with an Epigram in Verse Adapted to Each.* Scribner, 1940. Ages 9–12.

Edgeworth, Maria. *Simple Susan, and Other Tales;* il. by C. M. Burd. Macmillan. First published in 1800. (Children's Classics.) Ages 9–11.

Folmsbee, Beulah. *A Little History of the Hornbook.* The Horn Book, Inc., 1942. Age 12 on.

Lucas, E. V., comp. *Forgotten Tales of Long Ago;* il. by F. D. Bedford. Stokes, 1906. (Fine Art Juveniles.) Ages 9–12.

Lucas, E. V., comp. *Old Fashioned Tales;* il. by F. D. Bedford. Stokes, 1905. (Fine Art Juveniles.) Ages 9–12.

McClintock, Marshall. *Here Is a Book;* il. by Ninon MacKnight, and with photographs. Vanguard, 1939. Gives in considerable detail the various processes through which the author's own manuscript passed from its earliest stages until it was bound and ready to be sold. Ages 12–15.

McClintock, Marshall. *Millions of Books: The Story of Your Library.* Vanguard, 1941. The story of libraries from the smallest collection to the Library of Congress. The reader is taken behind the scenes and shown what goes on in the different departments. Ages 10–15.

Taylor, Jane and Ann. *Little Ann, and Other Poems;* il. by Kate Greenaway. Warne. Poems were first published about 1803, pictures for this edition made about 1883. Ages 9–11.

CHAPTER LXX

About Books and Reading

Becker, May Lamberton. *Adventures in Reading.* Lippincott, 1927. Friendly, informal talks on books and reading filled with a contagious enthusiasm. Many kinds of books are discussed, and there are book lists at the ends of the chapters. Ages 12–15.

Duff, Annis. *"Bequest of Wings"; a Family's Pleasures with Books.* Viking, 1944. This book tells of one family's experiences with books. Written with charm and humor, it is full of suggestions as to how children and parents may enjoy reading, art, and music together.

Eaton, Anne Thaxter. *Reading with Children.* Viking, 1940. Specific comment on more than 1000 children's books. Some of the chapters are: "Reality and Imagination"; "Poetry"; "The World's Great Stories"; "Round About the Earth"; "Men and Manners of the Past"; "Our World"; "Art and Music." Each chapter finishes with a check list of books mentioned in it.

Hazard, Paul. *Books, Children and Men;* trans. from the French by Marguerite Mitchell. The Horn Book, Inc., 1944. A distinguished French scholar discusses with brilliancy, sympathy, and evident enjoyment, children's books in relation to national traits and the cultures of various people. Age 15 on.

Moore, Anne Carroll. *My Roads to Childhood; Views and Reviews of Children's Books.* Doubleday, 1939. Inspiring comment on children's reading and books old and new by an authority. There is a list of representative books published between 1926 and 1938 and an essay on trends and developments in children's books during that period.

Richards, Laura E. *What Shall the Children Read;* il. by C. B. Falls. Appleton-Century, 1939. The author discusses the books, stories, and poems a child should know, from babyhood on, with delightful freshness and enthusiasm.

Sawyer, Ruth. *The Way of the Storyteller.* Viking, 1942. The author writes of storytelling as a folk art and tells of her own experience in "digging back" into the beginnings of race expression. There is practical help as well as inspiration for the storyteller, and eleven stories for telling are included.

Index

234 INDEX